SPADEWORK

LAYING FOUNDATIONS WITH 52 MEN FROM THE BIBLE

CARL BEECH

SPADEWORK by Carl Beech

Published by Scripture Union, 207–209 Queensway, Bletchley, MK2 2EB, UK
e-mail: info@scriptureunion.org.uk
website: www.scriptureunion.org.uk

Scripture Union Australia: Locked Bag 2, Central Coast Business Centre, NSW 2252
www.su.org.au

ISBN 978 1 84427 259 4

First published in Great Britain by Scripture Union 2007. Reprinted 2008.

British Library Cataloguing-in-Publication data: a catalogue record for this book is available from the British Library.

Cover design by Phil Grundy

Internal page design by Creative Pages: creativepages.co.uk.

Printed and bound in India by Thomson Press Limited.

CVM

Christian Vision for Men exists to equip the church to introduce every man in the UK to Jesus Christ. Concerned with all issues relating to men and the Christian faith, the organisation motivates, trains, teaches and equips churches to win men to the Christian faith and keep them gripped and excited by their relationship with Jesus.

Scripture Union is an international Christian charity working with churches in more than 130 countries providing resources to bring the good news about Jesus Christ to children, young people and families – and to encourage them to develop spiritually through the Bible and prayer. As well as coordinating a network of volunteers, staff and associates who run holidays, church-based events and school Christian groups, Scripture Union produces a wide range of publications and supports those who use their resources through training programmes.

WHAT OTHERS HAVE SAID ABOUT THIS BOOK...

Spadework opens the ground to the good seed of scriptural truth for twenty-first century men. Written intelligently, biblically and relevantly, it brings God's Word straight into our world.

John Glass, General Superintendent, Elim Pentecostal Churches

Carl Beech uncovers some tough men from the Bible and challenges men today to stand up for their faith in ways that are just as uncompromising and world-shaping!

J.John, author, international evangelist and speaker

What a refreshing read! Carl has described the experiences of 52 men we read of in the Bible making them relevant and challenging for Christian men. I highly recommend this great resource.

Lyndon Bowring, Executive Chairman, CARE

These biblical insights into how the Lord calls, inspires and uses men will be really helpful in advancing the Church's mission among men. I wholeheartedly commend this series of studies and pray they will enhance contemporary church life.

Rob Frost, Share Jesus International

When I began to read this book, the first emotion that hit me was a profound sense of relief. At last, someone is writing a book for men that isn't waffly, super-spiritual or fake. Carl is honest about his failings, and I can identify with his delusions about himself. He goes to the heart of these men in the Bible in such a way that in a few lines I feel I understand them. I know what they're about, and I feel close to them. They're blokes like me, not figures in stained glass windows, nor are they romantically garbed figures from the Romantic past of the Middle East. They're men like the men I meet with day by day, with one exception: every one of them has met the living God in a way that is real, and is making a real difference to their lives. If you are complacent, and want to stay that way, don't read this book. It'll be dangerous to your health. But if, like me, you have a secret longing for God to be more real, and his Spirit to touch you and remake you, then grab this book, read each short chapter. Let it sink in. Let it dig deep into you. There is every chance that you could be radically changed.

Eric Delve, Area Dean of Maidstone, international evangelist and conference speaker,
founder of the Detling Bible Camp

A bit about Carl

Carl, more commonly called Beechy, is Essex boy born and bred. At 18 he met Jesus. Deciding that day not to pursue a career in the armed forces because 'God was calling me to fight a different sort of battle', he went to uni and studied building. But after three years working in sales in a bank in the West End of London, he walked out – convinced that God was calling him to plant a new church. With no promise of income and no clue about how to run a church, Carl and his wife Karen set one up on an Essex estate where they experienced at first hand the power of God to change lives radically. After some years of that and then some youth pastoring – 'great fun' – Carl became senior pastor of a large church with several congregations – '90 per cent fun'.

Next, God called Carl to work towards seeing men across the UK turn to Jesus, which meant a move in 2006 to Bath as the National Director for Christian Vision for Men (CVM).

Carl and Karen have two girls, Emily and Annie. In his spare time he enjoys being with his family, goes fishing, cycles, walks his German Shepherd dog in the mud, lifts weights, eats curry and mourns the sale of his motorbike.

Thanks from Carl...

I want to thank in a big way...

- Karen, Emily and Annie for being patient with me when I have shut myself away from them to get some typing done. You must have got so tired of hearing me say, 'I just need to do a bit more work... ' Thanks, family. Let's have a big Chinese takeaway and I promise to watch a chick flick with you.
- The guys at CVM for giving me time out of the office to write this; and for your godly support and prayers. It's an honour and a privilege to serve with you. I thank God for your ongoing passion to see men won to Christ. Your energy inspires me. Let's keep running...
- My ex co-workers and still brothers at Billericay Baptist Church, who helped me learn so many lessons through my time there. Much of what we talked about at our weekly team meetings – which I really miss – especially the big lunches! – and elders meetings is found in these pages.
- Lin Ball who edited this and had a nightmare with my grammar. The team at Scripture Union are so committed to seeing God's Word come alive to people. Pray for them.
- My mum and dad, who always taught me that I could accomplish anything if I put my mind to it and put the effort in. Love you both; praying for you daily.
- Finally... thank you, Jesus, for meeting with me when I was 18. Life has been one incredible adventure ever since.

INTRO

I once fulfilled a boyhood dream and brought an old MGB roadster.

Then I sold it.

Bit lacking in detail, I know. Basically, apart from reading that I had an MGB, you don't really **know** about the whole experience.

There's so much I haven't yet told you. You don't **know** it was a rare 1973 automatic. You have no idea how much I paid for it (£2650). No clue that it had hardly any rust; that the engine had been rebuilt from scratch **and** was in show condition. You don't have the faintest idea that I sold it for more than I bought it for and that I regretted selling it ever since. You don't **know** the feeling of exhilaration I got when I really opened her up. Or the details of a highly memorable drive from Essex to Exeter – pedal flat to the floor all the way there and back, the stereo pumping out Oasis and the Beatles at full blast. You don't **know** how I used to feel, every time I got in it and smelt the old leather and heard the burble of the exhaust…

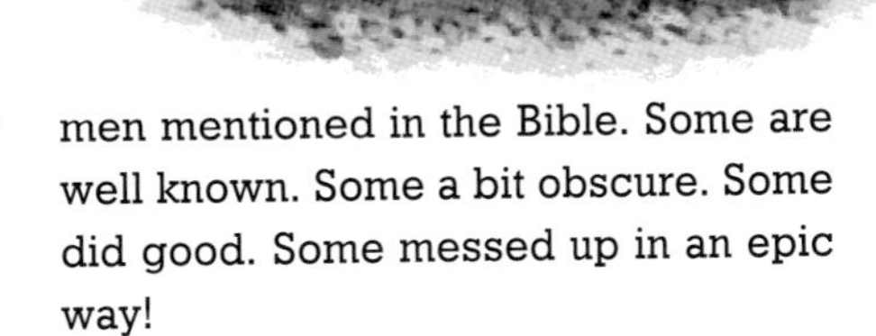

Now we're talking, right? After just a few more lines you are getting under the surface of my MGB experience!

Studying the Bible can often feel the same as reading my opening line.

Often we don't get a lot of information and, on the face of it, we don't get the inside track. So we need to get under the skin of the passage.

Throughout this book we are going to be getting under the skin of 52 or so men mentioned in the Bible. Some are well known. Some a bit obscure. Some did good. Some messed up in an epic way!

The aim of the book is two-fold:

1 We can learn some life lessons from others who have gone before

us, from their successes and their failures.

2 Character studies are a cool way of learning how the Bible hangs together. I'll be giving you some background to help you see how it all fits.

Here's a confession. When I became a Christian at 18, I knew so little about the most important book in the world that I used a book of children's Bible stories. I want to spare you the indignity! Some of the character studies are more factual than others. Some take one or two points and draw out some lifestyle lessons that help us go on with God.

I've written it with busy lives in mind. I know your struggles with balancing work and family and everything else that claims your attention. You should be able to read most of these character studies in 15 minutes or less. Ideally, read this book alongside an open Bible, checking out the verses I give you.

Some people have asked how I have chosen the 52 men. I just made a list and thought about what they had to say to men today. Some men had to be missed out. I can't tell you why Jonah is missing, other than to say that I felt it was more important to include Bezalel and Mephibosheth. Who? Read on and find out…

Fifty-two? Well, you could read just one a week and spend time chewing it over. Or demolish the whole book in a fortnight. You could study it with your men's group or read it on the train. It's up to you. Read it consecutively or randomly (that tends to be my reading style!). Some bits may make you hot under the collar; others will make you smile. Importantly, determine to get serious with God through reading it.

To all you smart Bible students out there: I own up, this isn't a deep work of scholarship. Yes there's some supposition and, yes, I make some assumptions and sweeping statements! This is a book about heart and character. Having said that, I've tried to be as accurate as I can. Trust me: I'm a pastor!

Finally, don't assume just because I dish out loads of life lessons that I have it all sorted myself. I don't. But I do know what I **ought** to be doing and how I **ought** to be behaving.

We're all in this together!

1

Who? **The first man**
When? **Ages ago!**
Why? **Because sulking can be a man thing**
Where? **Mainly Genesis 2 and 3**

ADAM

We start with the first man that ever set foot on the planet: Adam.

The story of Adam is a bit like the MGB issue (see my Intro)! The hard facts of his life don't come to more than around 50 verses in the whole Bible, ending with this less than detailed verse: 'Altogether, Adam lived 930 years, and then he died' (Genesis 5:5).

Hardly touchy-feely, is it? Imagine that at a funeral: 'Dave lived 73 years and then he died. That's it. Amen.'

I think if I conducted a funeral like that I would be defrocked. Or whatever the equivalent is for a non-frock-wearing Baptist pastor.

After reading the verses about Adam, you still don't know what he was like as a man.

- What did he like to eat?
- What did he do to relax?
- What was his favourite animal? (The sabre-toothed tiger?)
- We don't even know what he looked like. Most novels do describe their characters. (Craggy face? Smelling of *Old Spice*?) We need some detail to relate to characters we read about. So let's think way outside the box for a few minutes...

ADAM

From his first breath Adam was completely clean and pure. I'm not talking skin deep. I'm talking heart deep! Unlike us, he wasn't born into sin. He started with a clean sheet. He then went on to live for an incredible 930 years! That's some life. Here's two things to grab you:

1 Unlike Adam, we are born into sin. We have absolutely no idea what it would feel like to be completely pure. Sin busts us up mentally, emotionally and physically. We've had centuries of its effects on our lives. Not so for Adam. So maybe he was the ultimate man? Maybe our love of superheroes comes from the fact that the first man was one? Maybe deep inside there is a remnant memory of what we could have been – or, indeed, were meant to be?

   We can only speculate at the range of abilities Adam might have had. Perhaps he had the strength of Geoff Capes (remember him?), the speed of Muhammad Ali, the focus of Michael Schumacher, the height of Robert Wadlow and the brains of Stephen Hawking. I reckon that any meeting with Adam would have been an awesome experience. If we were to meet a man like him, we would want to call him 'sir'. We would be overawed by his physical presence and silenced by the speed of his thinking. The ultimate man? Just maybe!

2 Nine hundred and thirty years of life is staggering. To put it in perspective, we've come from the first powered flight to hypersonic aircraft in only a hundred or so years. Nowadays, going supersonic is as special to us as microwaving a ready meal – and even that's only been possible for about 25 years. The implications of such a long life are mind-blowing. How much knowledge could you accumulate in a life that long? How many experiences would you go through? Can you even **grasp** what it would have been like to have walked with God like a friend?

So what can we learn from Adam? Well, get this. For the biggest part of nine centuries, Adam lived with the knowledge that he had been cast from God's presence and had lost paradise...

And I'm wondering... was Adam a sulker? Did the ultimate man become the 'typical' man when sin entered the world?

I was once given a going-over by my boss when I worked in financial sales in London. It hurt. It was as far as you can get from soft, fluffy and pastoral. Bruising and brutal was more like it. The guy ripped into me, slamming his desk with his hands and pointing a finger right in my face. To add insult to injury, I was a fall guy for someone else and the injustice of it burned deep. And my response? At that stage, at 21 years of age, what did I do?

I went into a sulk.

Men are good at sulking. We've developed a head of expertise in the area.

Frankly, when a man sulks and indulges in chronic self-pity, it's an ugly sight. There's nothing worse than a grown man acting like a sulky teenager. But that's what I did. I sulked for England. I sulked to my girlfriend. I sulked to my parents. I sulked with my mates over a beer. And after all that, I sulked and skulked a bit more.

So, what did Adam do exactly, when the wheels came off in a massive way?

Did the man who once walked with God in the garden, who knew an incredible intimacy with him, who had the opportunity to live a life we can only dream about, **sulk**?

The Bible is pretty good at pointing out where people went wrong but, apart from the painful description of the meal to end all meals, we are not given that kind of information about Adam. Forced into exile from God's presence and facing a future of hard graft and misery, it does seem that Adam got on with it, whether or not he had a sulk first. The way the story is told paints a picture of a man who knew he had messed up but got on with making the best of a very, very bad situation.

Adam lifted up his head and got on with the job.

I'm sure he felt wounded, bruised, battered and cut to the heart. I'm convinced he would have wrestled long term with all kinds of grief and regret.

Think about the world he walked into outside Eden. After his disobedience to God even the animals would have been touched by sin. Those who were once pets and companions became predatory. Basically, Adam was now potential supper for the marauding sabre-toothed tiger that was once his pet! To add to the problems, the land started to produce weeds and thorns, offering him nothing but back-breaking sweat and toil. Spadework! Check it out in Genesis 3:17–19.

Perhaps the biggest issue Adam had to deal with was that he now faced the prospect of a body that would grow old and decay. Devastating! He wasn't originally designed to die and wear out, to get arthritis, go bald and come up with stock phrases like, 'I'm getting too old for this…'

He had been designed to be with God in paradise forever.

Adam now lived with the knowledge of paradise lost in more ways than one. An utter tragedy. He didn't even know that the one we call 'the second Adam' (Jesus) would come and deal with the problem of sin that he and Eve had set running. I imagine him just putting his shoulder to the plough and pressing on. That's the kind of man I want to be!

I think we allow ourselves periods of sulking because we think it won't matter, or simply because we can get away with it. Adam had no such luxury. A few months' sulking could have cost his life in the harsh environment he suddenly found himself in.

Us guys need to remember we are Jesus' witnesses. A sulking believer is more than just a wet blanket. Such childish behaviour could turn people off what we believe. Think about that. The reality is, we have no time for the luxury of sulking.

QUESTIONS

- How do you respond when the wheels come off?
- Do you spend your life looking back at what might have been? Or do you get on with it and make the most of what's in front of you now?
- Are you a sulker? Or a soldier? If you're married, ask your wife what you're like. Otherwise, ask your closest friend. Just don't sulk when you get the answer!

ACTIONS

- When you feel tempted to quit, grit your teeth and lift up your head.
- Stay thankful in all circumstances. That way, you won't live a life of regrets or envy.
- Specifically, thank God daily for Jesus. Because of him, paradise is returning!

2

Who? Visionary and faithful man of God who survived the flood
When? Pre-history
Why? For insights about radical faith and obedience
Where? Genesis 6–9

Noah

Let's set the scene.

One day an angel of God or an audible voice from heaven – take your pick – tells you to build a spaceship capable of carrying your family and all the animals in Bristol Zoo into space. You are to build it in your back garden and get all your supplies from the local hardware shop.

At which point in the day would you go and see your GP?

To put Noah's task in perspective, it was to build an enormous boat using local materials, with the aim of storing two of each kind of animal for a year – a task that was every bit as outlandish for Noah a few thousand years ago as it would be for you to build a spaceship now.

It's an absolutely staggering story of faith and belief. And a story that's been misused.

I believe its been massively diluted by its use as a children's story.

When I first went to church at 18, I had a row in a Christian bookshop because I couldn't believe that the only books you could get on Noah's ark were kids' stories! I remember telling the staff that they were out of order. How could you sell a book about mass destruction and death to kids? As a newbie in the Church I couldn't get my head round it. Still can't, actually. Noah's story is one of gut-churning horror, triumph over adversity, heroic faith, dogged grit and determination. Tough stuff.

NOAH

It's not for the faint-hearted, and definitely not the children's bedtime story we have made it.

Noah was a man of faith who stood rock solid in God in a time when no one else could be bothered or had the guts to. He honoured God when everyone else chose to ignore him. He stood his ground, probably under extreme ridicule. He glimpsed the bigger picture and saw the job through to the end, despite the cost to his reputation and livelihood.

Let's get rid of the fluff. Noah lived in a time when God moved in devastating holy power and judgement in a way we won't see again until Jesus comes back.

The story also contains what is possibly the saddest verse in the whole Bible: 'The LORD was grieved that he had made man on the earth, and his heart was filled with pain' (Genesis 6:6).

Noah lived in a knife-edge time. Everything around him was spinning out of control. Violence was endemic; the atmosphere dark and oppressive; hedonism ruled. Sounds familiar? But Noah remained blameless.

You and I know how hard it is to keep pure. You know how hard it is not to look where you shouldn't look and not to go where you shouldn't go. You know how hard it is not to stumble into lust, or allow anger to rise up, or let bitterness and revenge take hold of you. Noah fought those same battles and won. Probably through gritted teeth.

Was there a secret to his ability to remain distinctive? Look at Genesis 6:22: 'Noah did everything just as God commanded him.'

That's the key to being **righteous**!

Have you got that quality?

I'm talking about a steely determination to go where God sends you and do as he tells you – no matter what! Are you out of that mould?

Now think about a few of the facts. When Noah is first mentioned he was 500 years old. When Noah entered the ark he was 600! We don't know at what point (between Genesis 5:32 and 6:14–21) he got his orders. But it may have taken **up to 100 years** to build the ark! Details aside, this was a long journey of unrelenting faith, single-minded focus and perseverance.

NOAH

Bear with me for a couple more facts.

Noah got on board the ark on the seventeenth day of the second month (Genesis 7:11–13). He got out on the twenty-seventh day of the second month of the following year (Genesis 8:14,15). Now that's some test of a man's mettle! That's 370 days of waking up every day in a foul, stinking, messy wooden box, wondering if you will ever get out… wondering if you will ever see life on solid ground again.

I expect there were domestic tensions. I expect they all got up each other's nostrils at times as much as the stench did. Certainly Noah had his flaws. He probably spent the 370 days with dirty hands and a sore back. But he stuck at it!

Follow that.

QUESTIONS

- Do you have anything like the grit of Noah?
- Do you do all God commands – despite threats of ridicule or embarrassment?
- Do you see a vision through over the long term?
- Are you resistant to the pressures around you?
- When you face ridicule for your faith, how do you respond?
- Are you a man who grieves God? Or a man who gives God joy?

ACTIONS

- Learn from a man who got it right when the chips were down.
- Make a decision to be God's man and not a crowd follower.
- Make a decision to see a job through, no matter what.
- Learn to focus not on what people think about you… but on what God thinks about you.

3

ABRAHAM

Who? **Adventurer, father of the faith**
When? **About 2000 BC**
Why? **Never say never! He didn't quit believing God**
Where? **Most of Genesis 12–25**

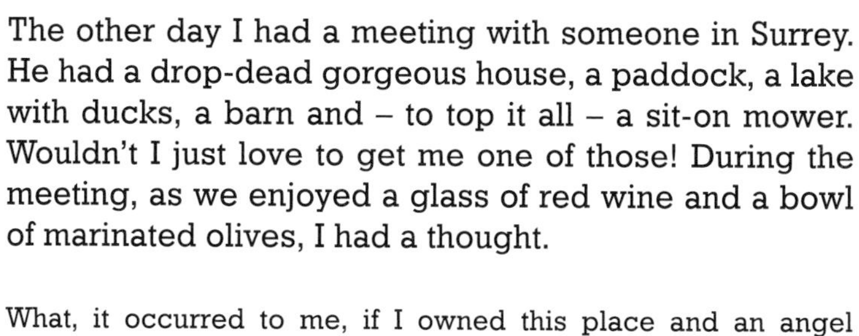
The other day I had a meeting with someone in Surrey. He had a drop-dead gorgeous house, a paddock, a lake with ducks, a barn and – to top it all – a sit-on mower. Wouldn't I just love to get me one of those! During the meeting, as we enjoyed a glass of red wine and a bowl of marinated olives, I had a thought.

What, it occurred to me, if I owned this place and an angel suddenly appeared and told me to pack up a few things and never come back?

What if I was told I had to leave it all behind and not even know where I was going? To add to the confusion and trauma… imagine I was newly retired, feet up and enjoying the spoils of years in business!

Would I go? Would I cry? Would I protest? Would I argue to take the sit-on mower?

Abraham had an incredible life. The way he tackled the dilemma of leaving everything behind has always inspired me.

'Leave it all,' God told Abraham (Genesis 12:1).

Grab hold of the implications of this…

You are 75 years of age. You've had a good crack at life and now you are drawing your pension, enjoying the fruit of your labours. And, suddenly, cutting through it all, God calls you to 'go'. Leave it all. Not only that, but the call comes in such a way that you are left in no doubt that there are whole chapters of your life yet to be written. Some of it will be spent in hardship; much of it without a clear sense of the end goal. You know deep inside that you will see triumph and disaster.

What would you do? He went for it!

People in Abraham's time were nomadic. Life was difficult compared to ours. They didn't know the comforts that we have. Zero refrigeration, no Sky TV, no dentists, chemists, Sudafed, or insurance policies against critical illness. They were hardened; tougher than we are and used to being on the move. And so, in one sense, Abraham was cut out to receive his marching orders. However, we have to acknowledge that it's always a wrench to leave behind everything that you know and love and are familiar with.

You see, human nature tends to want to settle. We pitch our tent somewhere, decorate, keep our heads down, occasionally seeking a bigger tent in a nicer part of town if we can afford it – and sometimes even when we can't!

Abraham was different. He spent time in the desert place, striving and pioneering, obedient to God's call despite the cost.

Somewhere along the way, most of us have lost that sense of adventure and pioneering. When God calls, we often find reasons not to go or to soften the instruction with a fluffy get-out clause. We may not all be called to employment in a church or ministry but I do believe passionately that we are all 'priests' in the biblical sense of the word and we all have a calling to adventure with Jesus.

The thing is, I also believe that God graciously allows us to choose. We can take the more comfortable path and he still works through us and with us when we do. However, I am utterly convinced that we are more likely to experience more of God when we maintain a pioneering spirit and a willingness to enter the desert.

As for me, given the choice, something stubborn in me always wants to take the hardest path! And my experience so far has been that it's worth it – every time!

At the age of 24, I was given the choice either to train as a pastor in the comfort of a large church, or to pioneer a new one on a tough estate down the road. Karen and I went for the second option. At times it nearly broke us. Certainly I had a load of sleepless nights and shed more than a few tears. However, it was also a time when we saw the power of God at work close up.

I remember one time when a guy about six foot seven came round to beat me up for telling people in his family about Jesus. While he confronted me in the kitchen, I tried to act calm and went to put the kettle on. (A cunning attempt at distraction!) When I turned around, he was cowering in the corner in a foetal position, shaking like a leaf. Needless to say, I was a bit perplexed. I was shocked when I asked him what was going on and got this answer back: 'There's power coming from you and I can't get near you.'

Just for the record, I felt nothing except stress!

Enter the desert, take the hard path – and see the Lord at work. I look back now in complete wonder at some of the stuff we saw God do, and I'm grateful for every tough moment.

If God asked me to do it again, would I go? Too right, I would!

Which road will you travel? Will you go where God leads you and do what he asks you? Or choose the more comfortable route?

Are you thinking that you're at the end of your adventure, that you have served your time? Think again. It's never over until the day we are called home.

QUESTIONS

- What path will you take?
- Dare you enter the desert, if called?
- Do you trust God with your family? Your finances? Your future?

ACTIONS

- Spend time thinking over the times you have felt God call you to a task or a move. Be honest with yourself. Were there times when you made excuses? Is there deep down a burning desire to break out of the comfort zone? Only you and God know. Do some business with the Lord.
- Ask a friend to pray with you about the issues.
- Remember this: God always finishes what he starts – as long as we are willing! I know this both from God's Word and my own experience. Live the adventure!

4

Who? Grandson of Abraham, a wrestler
When? About 1850 BC
Why? He responded to discipline and lessons like a man should
Where? He takes up a huge chunk of Genesis from midway through chapter 25

Jacob

One of the best things about the Bible is that you often come across characters that show us there is hope for us all. If you want to read about a guy like that, Jacob's your man! To get to grips with Jacob we need to start with a rapid tour through his life:

- His name means 'he grasps the heel' or 'he cheats'.
- He had a twin brother called Esau, who was a hunter and a real outdoors type.
- His dad Isaac had a real soft spot for Esau.
- His mum Rebekah had a real soft spot for him.
- Jacob stole what was Esau's by virtue of being the firstborn – giving Jacob more material wealth.
- Jacob had to do a runner from Esau! (Check out Genesis 27:41–45.)
- He was 40 when he set up home alone.
- He had a life changing dream in Bethel where he wrestled with God, admitted defeat and made an oath to him (Genesis 28:10–22).
- The fight left him with a permanent limp.
- His name was changed to Israel.
- He was reconciled to his brother but wisely choose to lead a separate life!

Jacob's is an up and down roller coaster ride of a story. He's left crippled and weakened in his body after wrestling with God but hugely strengthened in his faith. And here's the good news that comes out of it: God chooses us not on the basis of what we are, but on what we can become!

Jacob's whole life was one long process of messing up, getting disciplined, putting things right and growing from the experience. Whatever he sowed, he reaped. Nothing he did wrong slipped through the net. He learned the hard way! He had free choice as to which way he went, and made some bad choices. However, we know that God was always there, watching over him.

It's the same for each one of us. Read Psalm 139 if you have any doubts about that! It may seem that God is distant sometimes, especially when your back is against the wall or you have just let yourself down… but he isn't. It's just that sometimes God chooses to let us grow the difficult way. He will let us rebel and find out that we reap what we sow in the hope that we will then grow from our experiences!

Then other times he intercepts us with a burning bush and speeds up the growing process. Jacob's interception was a fight by a river. However, for the most part, growing in character is a long process. In fact, it takes a lifetime! Whatever and however God does it, you can be sure that God will finish what he has started. Note that he is not afraid to let us go through tough times to sort out our character! How many tough times we go through depends on how quickly we learn the lessons and get closer to God. Learn from a man who learned the hard way.

QUESTIONS

- What do you learn about tenacity from Jacob?
- In what way does this story encourage you?
- How does his story apply to your everyday life?

ACTIONS

- Be a man who pursues God.
- When you mess up, learn from it. Dust yourself off and get going again.
- Always remember the bigger picture. God will finish the work he started in you.

5

Who? Favoured son of Jacob
When? About 1740 BC
Why? Kept himself pure – and knew when it was right to run!
Where? Another big chunk of Genesis – from chapter 39 through to the end

Joseph

There's no doubt that Joseph had something special going for him – and I'm not just talking about the Old Testament equivalent of a Versace coat! Thanks to a few songs and plays, the coat of many colours is pretty much what most people know him for, and that's a real shame. So we're going to get past the coat and get learning from a man who could be annoying and appear arrogant, but who displayed incredible self-discipline and never gave in to circumstances.

Joseph was the eleventh of Jacob's twelve sons, born to Rachel who just happened to be Jacob's favourite wife. So it follows that Joseph was Jacob's favourite son. Bad parenting by Jacob led to Joseph having more than a rough time at the hands of his brothers. My advice is to resist having a favourite son or daughter; it only causes long term hurt and rejection and does the siblings in.

Anyway, the coat – a gift to Joseph from his doting dad – makes an appearance in Genesis 37. As a result of that and consistently uneven treatment, his brothers get so fed up that they sell Joseph into slavery. OK, so Joseph relaying a dream to his brothers which suggested that he was superior and that they would all bow to him didn't help matters! But, in a sense, the rot had already set in by that time.

The adventure begins; in brief, Joseph goes from being a highly trusted slave in the house of a senior government official (Potiphar) in Egypt, to being unfairly placed in prison, to being second-in-command of the whole of Egypt. Some journey, eh?

Finally, his brothers (who thought he was dead) come across him in Egypt where they go to find food during a famine. Joseph had come up with the bright idea of storing food in Egypt after interpreting Pharaoh's dream warning about impending famine. The brothers bow to him, just as predicted by Joseph years previously.

Here are four lessons to deal with:

1 We know Joseph is young, good-looking and well built. Women fancy him – in particular, his boss's wife. Not good. But does Joseph – in his sexual prime and yet still immature – succumb and take her to bed? No! He holds his ground and resists.

He doesn't hold the line primarily because he respects his boss, although that's what he refers to first in Genesis 39:8. He holds the line because to bed the boss's wife would be an offence against God! And there was no way Joseph is going to hurt God when he knows that everything he hopes for in life depends on him.

Ultimately, whenever we fall, it's God we hurt; which is why in his psalm of confession after committing adultery and murder (Psalm 51) David tells God it is **only** against him that he has sinned...

Joseph has to resist more than once! Potiphar's wife doesn't let up on the poor bloke. In fact, she nags him for sex! In the end, there's only one thing for it. Joseph does a runner (Genesis 39:12).

Now, that's character! How easy would it have been to give in? After all, no one would ever know – would they? Of course, what you really are is what you are when no one else is looking. Joseph knew that God would see it all and that's what kept him pure.

Guys, you can be sure that if ever there's a time when everything is going well in life and God's favour is resting on you, that's when temptation will come over the horizon and it might well be in the form of a drop-dead attractive woman in a miniskirt. If that happens, run boys! Run to the hills and don't look back! That fleeting moment of physical pleasure could cost you **everything**.

Just have in mind two things. Firstly, it may be a test from God to see if you are ready for the next stage. Or, secondly, it could be sent from Satan to destroy you. In either case, run! I've seen many a good man destroyed because he took a second look. Don't join their ranks!

2 Did you know that when God's favour is on you it blesses everyone near you as well? Just as sin from one person can pollute an entire organisation or family, so faithfulness from one person can bring peace and blessing. Read it for yourself! Genesis 39 is clear on the matter. The faithfulness of Joseph brings a blessing on the whole of Potiphar's household. What implications does that have for a man of God who holds the line in a business or in his family in issues of moral and spiritual integrity? I'll leave you to draw your own conclusions.

3 The situation gets even worse for Joseph. Falsely accused of raping his boss's wife, he's thrown into the dungeon. Joseph **still** holds the line. He could have got the hump with God when he was thrown into prison. He could have decided to believe the lie that God had abandoned him. He could have turned away from developing into a good man. Instead, he chooses to walk the noble path. He faces his false imprisonment with dignity.

4 Joseph was, of course, vindicated in the end. He was even reconciled to the brothers that sold him out. Don't make the mistake, though, of thinking that just because it all happened within a few pages in the Bible that it happened quickly in real time.

Joseph was at least 37 when he met up with his brothers again. (He was 30 when he entered Pharaoh's service in Genesis 41:46 and then there was at least another seven years before the brothers turned up.) Given that he was first sold at about 17 years of age, that's **20 years** of dealing with rejection and hurt. A long time to dream of revenge and retribution. It would have been so easy for Joseph to put his brothers through a living hell and lose any chance of reconciliation.

Most of us men are good at plotting revenge. We are good at fantasising about the downfalls of our enemies. We relish the thought of seeing someone get what they deserve. We love TV programmes and movies that show justice being meted out to people. Plenty of best-selling novels involve violent revenge. However, listen up: **revenge and following Jesus are completely incompatible**. You've just got to leave feuds where they belong... consigned to history, wiped from the 'to do' list. As soon as Joseph saw that his brothers were genuine, that's what Joseph did – and it led to a beautiful future.

QUESTIONS

- How would you feel if you were wrongly accused? How would you handle it?
- How do you fight temptation? When is running the only solution?
- How do you deal with the desire to gain revenge?

ACTIONS

- Make it a habit to be first to apologise.
- Deal with long-term feuds before they spin out of control.
- Make a decision to stay faithful to God even when he feels absent.
- Run from sexual temptation… and don't look back!

6

Who? **Possibly the most humble man that ever lived; an example of power in meekness**
When? **In about 1446 BC, at the age of 80, he led the Exodus**
Why? **A masterclass in true power**
Where? **The whole 40 chapters of Exodus is his story**

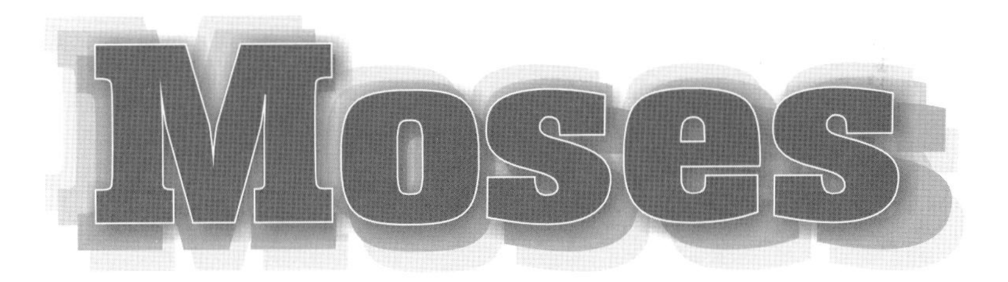

Moses was variously an orphan adopted into nobility, a murderer, a desert wanderer for 80 years, and perhaps the greatest leader the world has ever seen. Add to this the fact that he was so highly esteemed by God that God chose to speak to Moses face to face as a man speaks to his friend (Exodus 33:11) and you get the picture that his was no ordinary life. We call Wayne Rooney a hero (sure, he is a class act) and give knighthoods to men who make a few million. Well, Moses was a true hero – in every sense of the word. He took on the might of the Egyptian ruler despite hating the thought of public speaking. And he was no quitter:

- He led the people of Israel through a tough 40 years of grief.
- He put up with attempts on his life and almost constant aggravation and back-stabbing. But he stuck to the task.

What was Moses' secret?

It was his character!

There is a huge giveaway when we compare Exodus 11:3 with Numbers 12:3. The Exodus verse tells us that the Lord caused the Egyptians to consider Moses 'highly regarded' or 'considered a very great man' (New Living Translation). But Numbers 12:3 tells us that Moses was 'more humble than any man on the face of the earth'.

There is power in submission and greatness in humility.

Goes against the grain of the Alan Sugar school of leadership, doesn't it!

A man that is devoid of ego, who is rid of self-importance and arrogance, can be used powerfully by God.

Here's where the rubber hits the road. In order to die to yourself and develop the character of a man like Moses, there's only the hard way. There is no quick fix or instant formula. It can only come through the passing of time, through journeying the narrow way and collecting bruises and scars.

Consider this. We talk about the Israelites wandering in the desert for 40 years. We don't, however, talk about the 40 years Moses spent tending sheep alone before he became leader. Neither do we talk about the 40 years before that, which culminated in him murdering an Egyptian. (See Acts 7:23–30 and Deuteronomy 34:7.)

Probationary periods of 40 years? We get fed up with working six months on probation! When God appoints a great spiritual leader it comes after years of fashioning. When we appoint one, we send them to Bible college for three years!

All those years in Midian, alone tending sheep, taught Moses many lessons, especially about humility. As a result, he never thought too highly of himself.

Moses even gives us a masterclass in how to die well. He wasn't allowed into the Promised Land because of a momentary lack of faith and patience when he struck a rock to obtain water rather than speak to it (Numbers 20:11). However, when it was time to die, Moses marched up Mount Nebo and got a panoramic view of the Promised Land (Deuteronomy 34) and breathed his last. And there God buried him. When Moses died, we are told that his eyes were not weak, nor his strength gone. The meekest man on the face of the earth was also the mightiest, right until the end.

QUESTIONS

- What lessons in leadership does Moses offer you?
- What lessons do you learn about staying power and stickability?
- Are there areas of your character driven by ego and insecurity?
- Are you a meek man?
- What is true strength?

ACTIONS

- Resist pushing yourself forward too quickly.
- Embrace whatever desert experience comes your way. Too often we refer to those times as depressing. They needn't be. They can be times of personal growth.
- Practise humility by always finding a good word to say about others.

7

Who? **A craftsman**
When? **In the time of the exodus**
Why? **Because he was called and anointed to make stuff... a calling we don't always appreciate!**
Where? **Exodus 31:1–5**

Bezalel

You have probably never heard of Bezalel. If you have, great. But you are still probably wondering why he is in this book.

Well, it's simple.

His life demonstrates a key principle that I wish working men and church leaders would get hold of.

And it's this: it isn't just preachers and teachers of the Bible who are given a special job by God. God gifts and enables all kinds of people with all kinds of talents and skills in order to do all kinds of things. And that can include driving a van, making a table, filing some accounts or fixing an engine.

The fact is, that if the Israelites hadn't had a guy who was gifted at making stuff, then the tabernacle (the tent in which God was worshipped) and all the associated bits and pieces would have looked like something off *Blue Peter*, and that's without the double-sided sticky tape.

The principle is this: if you are good with numbers, then that gift is from God. If you are good at detail, that gift is from God. If you are good at fixing stuff, that gift is from God. If you are good at acting or music or poetry, they are from God. If you are good in business... you guessed it! That's from God.

BEZALEL

I work with a team of guys in an evangelistic organisation who all have diverse skills. When people deal with us, they seem to think that to be upfront speaking and teaching is the more spiritual gift.

Rubbish!

My teaching and training ministry wouldn't stand a chance if we didn't have good admin on the team. If one of my colleagues wasn't efficient at book-keeping and financial controls, we would soon shut down. If our techie team wasn't gifted and anointed, we wouldn't be able to put on a good conference.

If **you** are a Bezalel type, Exodus 38:22 is pretty key. Bezalel did **everything** as God asked, as told to him by Moses. I don't imagine he got shirty about his creativity or precious about it. He just got on with it, to please God. Remember that, all you creative and practical men out there! At heart, Bezalel was a servant. Not only that, but according to some Jewish writings, he was only 13 when he got the job. Amazing, isn't it? We really need to be raising up our younger men and letting them fly!

But back to 'anointing for practical work'.

Bezalel isn't the only one in the Bible to get this kind of mention. There are others who are remembered for their practical skills; like Tubal-Cain, the first toolmaker (Genesis 4:22).

I think at best we massively undervalue men with practical gifts and abilities. At worst we fail to realise these are gifts straight from the Father. The Bible says that Bezalel did all he did because the Spirit of God was on him.

I know a guy who can make just about anything from anything. He can turn his hand to fine art, building (and I don't mean a brick barbecue, I mean whole extensions), electrics, sculpting… the list goes on and on. The sad thing is that he always tells me he is searching for his calling in life. Perhaps the reason he doesn't realise he has found it is because we don't appreciate the amazing gifts he has.

Church leaders, hear my plea. When you get guys like my mate into your churches, give them a job and appreciate their gifts as if they come right from God. Because they do.

If you are one of the kingdom's incredibly anointed and gifted practical workers, then receive from the Father what he has given you and don't feel looked down on simply because you aren't a speaker or a worship leader. Your craftsmanship is an act of worship and a sure sign of the presence of the Holy Spirit in the world.

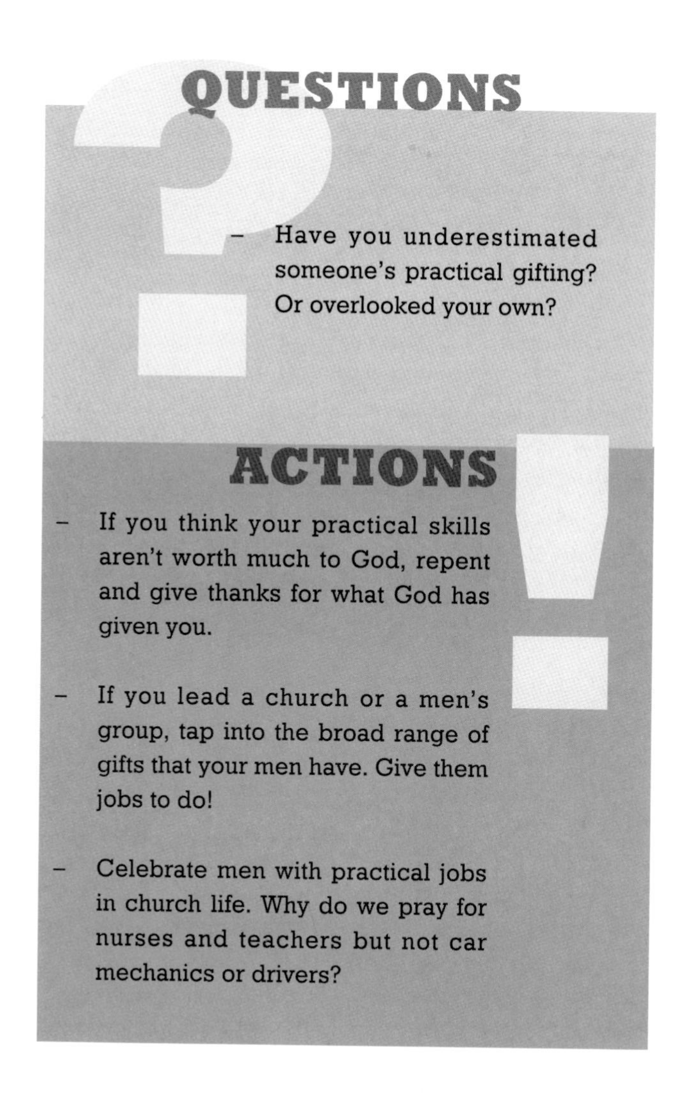

QUESTIONS

- Have you underestimated someone's practical gifting? Or overlooked your own?

ACTIONS

- If you think your practical skills aren't worth much to God, repent and give thanks for what God has given you.

- If you lead a church or a men's group, tap into the broad range of gifts that your men have. Give them jobs to do!

- Celebrate men with practical jobs in church life. Why do we pray for nurses and teachers but not car mechanics or drivers?

8

Who? Leader of Egypt, thought to be divine by his people
When? Same period as Moses: 1440ish BC
Why? Learn how not to lead...
Where? The heart of his story is in Exodus 6–12

Pharaoh

Now we have a masterclass in how not to do it!

Men are notorious for digging their heels in. We are past masters at being bloody-minded and stubborn. Often we refuse to budge even though it causes damage to people around us, whether at work or home. Well, Pharaoh, the mighty and feared leader – hailed as a god-like figure – found out the hard way that **pride is a lethal weapon**.

You know the story of the dreadful plagues God sent on the Egyptians when they wouldn't let Moses lead the Israelites out of slavery. Eleven times Moses and Aaron went to Pharaoh. On the last visit Moses was hot with anger! Pharaoh refused to listen, even though the threat this time was to the lives of all the firstborn of the great nation he led. God is patient and gracious but will only be pushed so far. Pharaoh was about to learn that there comes a time when you can overstep the mark when dealing with the God of Israel!

The resulting tragedy was a horror story of epic proportions. We can only assume what was going on in Pharaoh's mind during this whole process. I suspect he was like many of us. At first dismissive and in denial. Then doubts crept in. Then fear settled on him as the plagues got worse. Slowly, arrogance turned into deep insecurity. Outwardly, he appeared confident, dismissive. After all, having resisted so far it would be a major dent in his pride to give in at this late stage! He would want no one to think he was weak.

Have you ever behaved like that? Maybe you are the kind of man who never backs down in a row no matter what the implications. Pharaoh's story is a classic lesson for all time on what happens when a man lets his ego and insecurity get the better of him.

Men, we need to learn meekness. We need to guard against pride and make sure we don't walk as Pharaoh walked. Even after all the misery and hurt he caused his people, top of his agenda was to get revenge by hunting Moses down. You would have thought he had learned his lesson, wouldn't you? Before you nod in agreement, think about the times when you've behaved just the same way!

I believe the antidote is found in Philippians 2:3: 'Do nothing out of selfish ambition or vain conceit, but in humility consider others better than yourselves.' If we did this, our homes and our places of work would be far better places to be.

If you are currently digging your heels in... then dig 'em out! Jesus taught, 'Blessed are the meek, for they will inherit the earth' (Matthew 5:5). The proud? Well, they just come to ruin.

QUESTIONS

- Is pride always bad? For example, can a man have pride in a job well done?
- Do you fear God? Is it right to fear God?

ACTIONS

- Check yourself next time you are in a confrontation.
- Never be too proud to step back and ask forgiveness.
- Next time you find yourself digging your heels in... dig 'em out!

9

Who? **Sometime spy and future right hand man to Joshua**
When? **Another character from way back in the time of the exodus**
Why? **He had 'a different spirit' and followed God 'wholeheartedly'!**
Where? **Numbers 13:30–33; 14:24**

Caleb was a fighting man, one of the Israelite leaders from the tribe of Judah. Sent into Canaan with 12 other men, his task was to reconnoitre the land to check out if the Israelites (on the run from Egyptian slavery) could settle there. Having been promised a land 'flowing with milk and honey' the people were desperate to find a place they could finally call home.

The initial survey looked good. Plenty of fruit, fertile soil for farming. The land seemed to warrant the 'flowing with milk and honey' description.

But there was a problem. The people who lived there were bigger and hairier than they were. At least, that's what they thought. They even thought that the Nephilim – legendary people of giantlike proportions – lived there.

Only two men decided that they should go for it. Joshua and Caleb.

Caleb didn't see the giants, he saw the **possibilities**. He didn't see defeat, he had **faith** in God. In fact, 40 years earlier Joshua and Caleb had pleaded the case for invasion, only to be overruled.

Here's the amazing thing. The implications of the people succumbing to fear was not only a period of 40 years in the desert. Every adult alive at that time demonstrating a lack of faith died before they had another chance to enter the Promised Land. Only Joshua and Caleb remained alive. Joshua, of course, had the honour of leading the invasion force into Canaan.

Think about that. God let the people wander endlessly until every one of them had died, leaving only their ancestors to cross into the land! Scary stuff. I wonder how many times churches today miss out on God's blessing in the here and now because they fail to operate in faith and grab hold of an opportunity when it has presented itself.

- 'But it will cost too much; we don't have that sort of money.'
- 'Isn't it a bit risky?'
- 'Have we really got enough manpower to tackle this?'

I've heard it all over the years. It's no different from the spies deciding that it was too tough to cross over.

Yet Caleb had 'a different spirit' and followed God wholeheartedly – and that's the key to seeing God's blessing. We need to be people who exercise faith and expectancy. For too long men in churches have sat back and ignored their responsibility to stand up as Christian believers in their nation. For too long they have left it to their praying and believing women. Isn't it time the men of our day followed in the footsteps of Caleb?

Caleb was 85 when he conquered Hebron and set up home. Not bad going, eh? He certainly wasn't putting his feet up, thinking he was past it.

QUESTIONS

- What excuses have you made for shirking responsibilities?

ACTIONS

- Make a decision to trust God as a first response to a problem.
- Cultivate 'a different spirit' – one that's full of hope and sees possibilities.
- Remember that no giant is unbeatable with God on your side. I don't know what giants you are facing. If there aren't any right now, I'm certain that there will be one or two at some point in your life. Remember Caleb.

10

Who? Soldier, spy and leader after Moses
When? Around 1400 BC
Why? He was not a quitter, but a real 'can do' character with dogged trust in God
Where? He has a whole book in the Old Testament named after him

Joshua

...'without faith it is impossible to please God' (Hebrews 11:6).

Ever come across this 'hits you like a juggernaut doing 80 mph' verse?

Joshua's name says it all. It means 'Yahweh (God) delivers'. He was a man of considerable stature, befitting the one chosen to succeed Moses. Just imagine following in his footsteps!

Joshua was a battle-hardened soldier: fearless, loyal, determined and courageous. He had fought solidly against the Amalekites as the people journeyed through the desert and had been in the front line as Moses' general (Exodus 17:8–13). His willingness to serve loyally and without question under another man is a giveaway to his character. It's a key reason why God was able to use him later.

You can't have authority unless you place yourself under it!

The funny thing is, many men I meet who want to be leaders are the worst followers!

I have learned that to go further and deeper with God you need to be a man who can submit and place himself under authority. Every time I have gone to the next level in my faith, it has been after a period of learning humility!

In Joshua 1:16,17 you can see the response of the people when Joshua assumed command: 'Whatever you have commanded us we will do, and wherever you send us we will go. Just as we fully obeyed Moses, so we will obey you.'

That kind of obedience could be dangerous if given to a leader who was self-serving. Joshua, however, was a servant and only had the interests of the people at heart.

Perhaps the two most intriguing insights into his character come early on in his leadership at Jericho and at the river Jordan.

Jericho was a massively fortified city that the Israelites had to conquer. Instead of fighting, the Lord told Joshua to march around it with the armed men for six days and then on the seventh day to send seven priests around it seven times blowing trumpets. I wonder if Joshua felt just a tad insecure about that. It's hardly a classic battle plan.

The thing was, even before God gave the instructions, he said to Joshua: 'See, I have delivered Jericho into your hands… ' So, in a very real sense, it was already theirs. They just had to do what they were told. Joshua went for it without question – and, of course, the walls came 'a-tumblin' down'.

I wonder how many of us miss out on seeing God's best because we think we know a better plan. OK, so we may not have any cities to conquer. But the principle applies. Take, for example, our financial giving. Often we don't give to God because we think we haven't got enough money. However, many people have found that when we reverse our thinking to, 'Can I afford not to give to God?' then we see God's blessing flow into our lives. I have even seen people come out of debt when they started to honour God financially. Doesn't make sense – but then his ways are not our ways. I have found it better to trust God and take him at his word than follow my own schemes and plans.

So much for Jericho. What about the river Jordan? When Moses struck his staff into the water, they saw the waters part. When Joshua had to cross the Jordan, they actually had to step into the water first (Joshua 3:13,14).

How insecure did Joshua feel as the priests dipped their toes in the water? Especially as the Jordan was in flood at the time! Again, trust and obedience paid off and the waters parted.

JOSHUA

Sometimes, guys, we just have to step into the water.

When I felt God call me to my current job, accommodation was an issue. We had been living in a church house; the new job was 180 miles away; and there was no money in the organisation's bank account to pay me.

Karen and I were convinced that God had called us, so we put our feet in the water. So far I've been paid every month since we started and we live in a fantastic part-furnished house that God miraculously provided. God knows best and when you trust him you find that out. Our kids even got places in a brilliant school when we had been told there were absolutely no places available. That's not to say that God always works in this way, or does so immediately – but often his provision confirms his calling.

QUESTIONS

- If you have a boss, do you (like Joshua under Moses) fight for him – or are you watching for the opportunity to move in?
- Do you see possibilities or obstacles?
- Do you have courage and trust based on your knowledge of God? Or do you need to get to know him better?

ACTIONS

- Be a man who says 'why not?' instead of 'what if?'
- Choose to be a man of possibilities and hope, not obstacles and pessimism.

11

Who? **Soldier in the Israelite camp**
When? **During the period of Joshua's leadership**
Why? **It's all about obedience or, in this case, lack of...**
Where? **Joshua 7**

Achan

I'm amazed how few men know the story of Achan. Guys, this is one story in the Bible we have to take hold of. It's not a pleasant story – but stop and read it now.

Yes, it's a story that speaks for itself. I don't need to go over the finer points with you. But let me ask you a question. Have you ever known fear? I mean, have you ever experienced sheer abject terror?

I am absolutely convinced that in the aftermath of this event the people of Israel had a new fear of God.

They had been used to victory; they were used to the presence of God sending their enemies fleeing from them. They fought with few or no casualties and were used to seeing their enemies melt away with fear. And so, when it came to dealing with Ai there was a rather blasé attitude towards it all – 'Just send a couple of thousand men to take it... '

The rest you can read. They were routed and defeated. But not in the manner you might expect from their reaction.

Verse 5 tells us that only 36 men were killed. Get to grips with that. While any death is a tragedy, by modern or ancient combat standards, 36 men lost out of 3000 is pretty good going!

They were used to God's protection and blessing. And so, when it had gone, they really knew it!

Loss was a shock. Not the norm. The thing is, they were all exposed to danger because of the actions of one man!

There are profound implications for us. Take this on board! Your sin doesn't just have an impact on you. It has an impact on the people around you... on your church, your family, your friends.

Let's get really specific:

- Pornography is a chronic problem in the Church.
- Giving is hovering at around only three per cent of income across the Church.
- The Sabbath is no longer regarded as holy.

I could go on and on...

And we wonder why the Church is struggling! We wonder why it seems so hard to know and sense that God is with us!

There's a lesson to be learnt from Achan's sin. The next time you feel tempted, remember that it isn't just about you.

In Joshua's time, in order to rid the camp of the sin, Achan and all his family were stoned to death. No messing around. The cancer had to be dealt with, cut out quickly and incisively. You may think it brutal, but the integrity of the camp of Israel was at stake.

Thankfully, we have the cross! Thank God that we can approach him right now and deal with things that are blunting his presence. I thank God that a man died in my place so that I don't have to face the horrific consequences like Achan and his family did.

However, the onus is on us to deal incisively and surgically with any hidden sin that is blunting our edge and bruising our spirits.

Don't delay. Get real with yourself and draw close to God.

QUESTIONS

- How does it make you feel when you consider that no sin is hidden from God?
- How does it make you feel that God is so angered by sin?

ACTIONS

- As soon as you can, find a couple of men you can share with. Let them be the kind of men who will look you in the eye and ask if you are 'clean'. Be accountable to each other.
- Look at putting some accountability software on your PC.

12

Who? One of the judges who ruled Israel
When? About 1300 BC
Why? Sometimes you just got to seize the initiative...
Where? Judges 3:12–30

Ehud

The period of history that we know as the time of the judges is without doubt one of the most turbulent and violent found in the Bible.

It's packed with accounts of murder, sexual violence, anarchy and pure hedonism. The people would regularly turn from God and then find themselves spiralling out of control into anarchy. When you ditch God the rules go out of the window.

In the midst of the chaos, God would raise up a leader who would pull them out of the muck. At times God would use a heavy, a spiritual bare-knuckle fighter who could literally bang some heads together and slaughter the opposition. At other times God would use a man or woman who had just a bit more panache and cunning, to restore order from chaos.

Ehud was far from subtle. More of a kebab with chilli sauce sort of bloke than a canapés with foie gras fan!

His story is short and sweet and only comes to around 16 verses from first appearance to death. But it sure carries a lesson to learn. Let's start with the headlines:

- He was left-handed (as is the author and all true heroes).
- He was from the Benjamite tribe, which I find amusing, because the name means 'son of (my) right hand'!
- He ruled for 80 years and Israel was at peace all that time.

EHUD

Before Ehud appeared on the scene, Israel was under severe oppression from its enemies, particularly the Moabites led by King Eglon.

Ehud, being left-handed, straps his sword under his cloak on his right thigh where no one would expect it to be. He goes to the king with a tribute, pretends he has a secret message, gets himself alone with the king – and then runs him right through with the sword! **Game over and job done**.

The biblical account is more graphic. I'll say no more but encourage you to read it. So what on earth do we learn from this?

- Ehud was calm under pressure.
- He was decisive.
- He was not afraid of confrontation.

So, sometimes a man has to do what a man has to do. Note, however, that I'm not advocating assassination!

God can use a man for great things when he's prepared to overcome his fears and place his confidence in him. There are masculine traits that God has given us for a reason. We need to be prepared to use them for his purposes.

The fact that Ehud was able to keep the peace for 80 years shows clearly that he had qualities of leadership as well as good sword skills. As soon as Ehud died, the nation slipped back into despair and debauchery. What does this tell you about the effect of just one godly and decisive man on a nation?

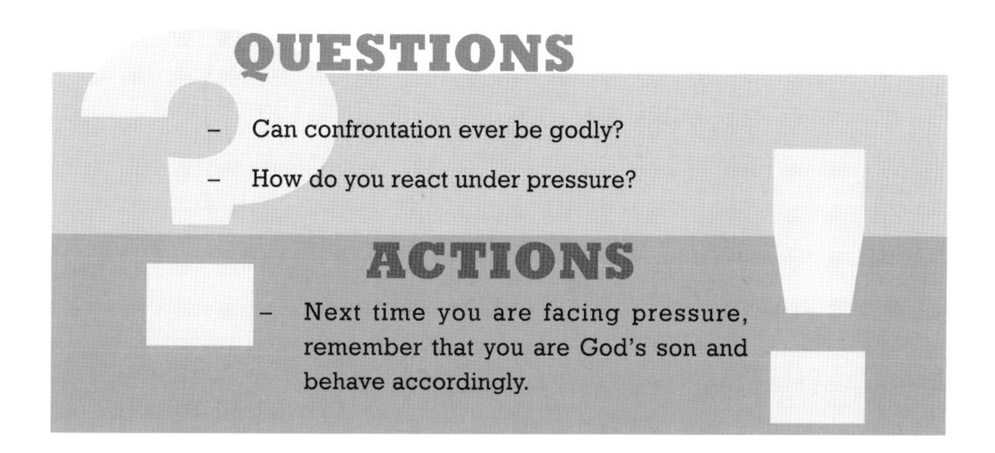

QUESTIONS

- Can confrontation ever be godly?
- How do you react under pressure?

ACTIONS

- Next time you are facing pressure, remember that you are God's son and behave accordingly.

13

Who? **A judge for 40 years**
When? **In the time of the judges of Israel**
Why? **A warrior and a hero, but a man who had his flaws**
Where? **Judges 6–8**

Gideon

A brief overview:

- Gideon's name means 'one who cuts down'.
- Even before his first battle he was hailed by an angel from God as a 'mighty warrior' (Judges 6:12).
- His main task was to wipe out the threat to Israel from enemies called the Amalekites and Midianites.
- Yes, there's a story about a sheep fleece!
- His life didn't end on a happy note – a much ignored fact!

Gideon was a complex guy. At some points he was seemingly fearless. At other times he needed constant reassurance due to some chronic insecurity. In fact, you could make a case from the fleece episode that what he is most famous for is attempting to get out of doing what God wanted.

The (in)famous fleece story occurs in Judges 6. Gideon was an unknown. He describes himself as the 'least' in his family, which was itself from the weakest clan! Someone like that doesn't just stroll into HQ and seize the leadership of the people. He seemed to be a nobody and one of life's losers. Hope for us all then!

Leadership for Gideon came the hard way. At that time the Israelites were worshipping an idol called Baal and not God. So, to put things right, there had to be a showdown. Under God's guidance as well as under the cover of darkness, Gideon smashed down the altar to Baal and put in its place an altar to God. The reaction was violent and Gideon faced the very real prospect of losing his life!

However, the leader in Gideon emerged. He fronted out an angry crowd issuing death threats and displayed real courage. So far so good.

However, when the reality of battle set in just a short time after, things started to go wrong. Even though God had displayed his power to Gideon by torching some meat and bread (6:20–22) and promising to be with him, Gideon twice laid out his fleece to **make sure** that God was really going to be with him. Once he lays it out to see if it will get wet on dry ground and the other time to see if it stays dry on wet ground.

Some of you may think this is fair enough.

I don't.

In fact, I want to suggest that this betrays a flaw in Gideon's character that comes to the surface later with destructive consequences.

The question I want you to consider is this: If God has spoken once, is that enough?

We might need reassurances in some of our **human** relationships. People say things and then have a terrible habit of letting us down. **But God**?

The late great preacher Charles Spurgeon said that 'to doubt God was a sin that was not to be tolerated'.

I'm with him on that one.

We are meant to reflect God's character. And God doesn't dither about. He isn't one to change his mind or back down from his word. We are called to model the same qualities, inspiring utter confidence in what we promise.

Now, of course, that doesn't preclude seeking counsel and checking what we believe God is saying against his Word. The difference is this: once we are clear that God has spoken – after seeking the counsel of other believers, praying and checking out the Bible – we should be prepared to act. Think about it:

- When God commanded Abraham to go – he went!
- When God told Noah to build an ark – he built!

- When God told Joshua to cross into the land – he crossed!
- When God told Gideon to go to battle – he… laid out a couple of fleeces…

See the difference?

In Gideon's defence, once he was sure, he really went for it. He went into battle against a massive army with only a few hundred men and no weapons. He routed anyone and everyone who stood in his way and really did live up to the meaning of his name. In fact, he and his men took out around 120,000 men and went on to defeat the remaining 15,000. It was a truly remarkable military victory.

While he's still listed as a hero of the faith, things then went horribly wrong for Gideon. I'm not sure whether it was ego, ignorance or just the impact of a flawed character. But he lost his way spiritually. He demanded the gold taken by the soldiers as plunder and built an ephod – a statue to worship – out of it. We aren't given reasons for this. I'm guessing that maybe Gideon wanted to build something to remind the people of the victory. But, because of the Israelites' tendency, given half a chance, to worship anything and everything, it led to spiritual meltdown. Ultimately it led his family astray and the whole of Israel too.

QUESTIONS

- Is your 'yes' really a 'yes'? Are you a man whose word holds good?
- Do you ever feel a need to lay out a fleece?
- Do you think that a fleece is a good way to check God's guidance? Or an example of weak faith?

ACTIONS

- Determine to be a man of unquestioning obedience to God.
- Build your trust in God by studying his character.
- Be bold in doing what God has told you to do.

14

Who? **Bare-knuckle fighter and testosterone-led judge of Israel**
When? **Around 1070 BC**
Why? **His story teaches us about when God says 'Enough is enough... '**
Where? **Judges 13–16**

Samson

Have a row with Samson and you were more likely to end up in a punch-up than negotiation. He was a bare-knuckle fighting warrior who relied more on brute force than persuasion. He was no diplomat. Certainly not the kind of man you would use at a United Nations summit on weapons reduction. But if you needed to storm an enemy position...

Earmarked from birth, Samson was a Nazirite. That's a man who took a vow to be in God's service. Sometimes these vows were for a period, rarely for a lifetime. But for Samson the promise was for life. That meant the stringent following of a lifelong code of behaviour:

- His hair was to be uncut.
- Zero wine/alcohol or even any food made of grapes and raisins.
- No contact with the dead.

For the lowdown on the rules for being a Nazirite turn to Numbers 6:1–21.

Let's get right to the nitty-gritty of the story. Samson never really fulfilled his potential. From what we can see, he was really no more than a pain in the neck for Israel's enemies (the Philistines in this case). Probably he could have wiped them all out if he had been a little more focused and less obsessed with getting his own way and having a life filled with pleasure. He did the classic man thing, really – getting sidetracked and ultimately derailed by wine, women and himself. I wonder how many men miss the moment and don't do something great for the same reasons?

SAMSON

Don't make the mistake of the comic book versions of this story in thinking that the secret of Samson's strength was totally in his uncut hair. It wasn't! OK, so Delilah nags him to death and he **tells** her that it's all in the hair. And yes, he did lose his strength after his hair was cut. However, we mustn't forget to look at all the events that happened **before** Samson had his hair cut.

Have a quick scan of the Bible account right now:

- In Judges 14:8 he eats from a dead lion – forever immortalised on tins of syrup to this day!
- In Judges 14:10 he has a huge party that probably included drink.
- In Judges 16:19 he has his hair cut.

So, he's not doing too good on the Nazirite thing then, eh?

The amazing thing is God's grace in all of this. Even after breaking the first two of his vows, Samson's anointing of sheer strength remained with him.

There's a lesson in there somewhere.

I often wonder how pastors and speakers keep going with seemingly amazing ministries when it later turns out that they were committing adultery or getting addicted to booze for years in secret. Perhaps it's God's grace? Perhaps the gifts and anointing are given without condition? All I would say is that it would be a massive mistake to think that God is pleased with you just because you see some 'fruit' in your ministry or work. God could be very displeased with you despite apparent signs of success. A sobering thought...

However, as we always see with the Lord, there comes a time when he will simply remove his blessing because we have crossed the line. The cutting of Samson's hair was one step too far. The tragedy was that Samson was so wrapped up in himself that he didn't even notice God's blessing had evaporated (Judges 16:20) and his strength with it.

Amazing, isn't it, that he just didn't notice that God's presence had left?

I once knew a speaker with an amazing preaching gift. He took it for granted, stopped preparing and even took to preaching after having a few beers. One day he stood up to speak and the Lord just took the gifting away. He stood there like a lemon, apologised and left the platform. A salutary lesson. He didn't preach again for many years.

God is patient, merciful, gracious and full of love. But there comes a time when enough is enough. When that time comes, it's likely we will have slipped so far that we just don't notice that the Lord has left us because we've so completely numbed our spiritual senses.

Don't make the mistake of thinking that just because God's using you that you might not be skating on thin ice. History is littered with the stories of amazing men of God doing amazing things right up to the moment when their sin was uncovered and it all fell apart. Often it's then revealed that there was rebellion and sin going back years. We wonder how God could keep using these men! We wonder why God blessed their ministry! Well, the truth is that God will give us just so long to get ourselves sorted and then he removes his presence...

Samson came to a very sorry end – well, almost. Blinded, shackled, degraded and turned into a freak show... at the last he cried out to God. Because God is not only merciful but he always finishes the job, Samson was once again anointed with strength and in his dying moments pulled a whole building down on top of himself and a bunch of partying Philistines. In fact, as it says, 'he killed many more when he died than while he lived' (Judges 16:30).

QUESTIONS

- In what ways might you be displeasing God and blunting the anointing on your life?
- What does Samson's story teach you about repentance?

ACTIONS

- Carry out an audit of your personal life. Where are you pushing the boundaries? Is there anything you need to deal with right here and now?
- Remember that God always finishes what he starts. So it's never too late for a fresh direction.

15

Who? Last-ever judge, awesome priest and prophet
When? Around 1050–1000 BC
Why? Because listening to God is vital
Good or bad? Awesome!
Where? In two whole books of the Old Testament named after him, but mainly the first 16 chapters of 1 Samuel

Samuel

Samuel got his first mission from God when he was just a young boy and heard God speak to him – a very rare event that lets us know from the outset that this was one special guy.

In fact, Samuel had been dedicated to God by his mother Hannah before he was born. She had been crying out to God for a child (1 Samuel 1:9–11).

So the scene is set for an extraordinary life. From the child who hears the voice of God, Samuel grows into an anointed prophet and kingmaker who wielded massive influence over the nation of Israel.

At one stage in Israel's up and down history when the Philistines were a constant threat and the people had turned from God, it took Samuel to be appointed ruling judge for the nation to return to a secure footing. Then Samuel was used by God to appoint the first king, Saul. Saul may have been king but Samuel was the kingmaker and the real power in the nation as he was the one who walked with God and the one who set down the rights and responsibilities of kingship. In fact, Samuel's written regulations for kingship (1 Samuel 10:25) were to remain a tool that future prophets used to call to task future kings who went astray.

Later, when Saul went too far off the rails, it was down to Samuel to anoint and appoint David as his successor.

Samuel's position was clear. Whatever the man on the throne, he was the greater power behind the throne – an anointed man of God.

QUESTIONS

- How good are you at listening to God?
- Samuel was no respecter of persons. His first undivided loyalty was to God. What about you?

ACTIONS

- Be focused on God if you want to experience the anointing of God.

16

Who? First king of Israel, man of angst, possibly psychotic
When? About 1030 BC
Why? We need to know it's important to submit to God
Where? 1 Samuel 9–31

Saul

Saul started well. He was anointed by Samuel as the first king of Israel, at which point the Spirit of God powerfully rested on him to such a degree that people who had previously known him couldn't believe the change (1 Samuel 10:9–11)!

So it all looked promising at first: a new king, a new era. Plus the anointing of God. It was all there for the taking. However, he went downhill faster than a big bloke on a bobsleigh, and it wasn't pretty.

Now bear in mind that Saul was 30 when he became king and he held the position for 42 years. He was no fly-by-night or seven-day wonder. He had courage in battle and broad shoulders. That's never in question. **But what he lacked was an obedient spirit**. As a result he inflicted upon himself a life of complete and utter misery.

Put simply, it went pear-shaped for Saul because he didn't do as he was told. His reign was supposed to be under the authority of God's representative, the prophet Samuel – through whom God was still supremely in charge. Saul kept missing the point and had a blind spot the size of an elephant.

The first signs of things going wrong are when Saul, out of fear and impatience, offers a burnt offering instead of Samuel (1 Samuel 13:9–14). The consequences for that were harsh. Saul was told that his dynasty would be broken and that the Lord had sought out a man after his own heart (David). If you think that this reaction was a bit over the top, let me make this point. When God is looking for a leader, he looks for faith. God didn't want a man leading his people who had weak character and an inability to trust him, so he cut Saul away.

In fact, as you read through the story of Saul's life, you see just how spot on God was. When men of God mess up, plenty of them manage to put things right and not repeat the same mistake. But not Saul.

I know men like that. When their boss tries to help them understand where they might be going wrong, instead of taking it on the chin and dealing with it, they just get the hump and go from bad to worse. They refuse to listen, becoming deaf to constructive advice and blind to warnings.

That's what Saul was like.

And so, by chapter 15, we see the same old, same old. Tasked with completely wiping out the Amalekites (people and livestock), Saul bravely goes to battle. But then, seeing some nice juicy, plump calves and sheep, he promptly forgets his orders. In the face of demands from his men, he keeps the livestock and doesn't kill the king but takes him prisoner.

Bad move. He put pleasing his men above obedience to the voice of God.

Result? He is rejected as king, the Spirit of God leaves him and an evil spirit takes over instead. (1 Samuel 16:14). He spends the rest of his life battling rage, anger and depression.

Finally, consumed with jealousy towards David, he tries to kill him – even though he once loved him (1 Sam 16:21–23) – consults witches (1 Samuel 28) and ends up disembowelling himself on his sword, having witnessed the death of his sons. Not a Hollywood-style happy ending.

Some believers seem to live lives that are completely blessed. They go from mountain top to mountain top. When tough times come, they come through. In the storm, they keep their joy. Perhaps there's a reason why.

I think it's because they trust God and love him. They do as God wants and as a result God blesses them. Every faithful man in this book who lived an obedient life ended on a high note. That must tell us something.

QUESTIONS

- Why do you think men find it so hard to submit to God?
- What sort of church structure would help foster accountability and obedience to God?
- Is it right always to do as your boss tells you?
- How important is it to please other people?

ACTIONS

- Consciously put yourself under the authority of God and his anointed followers. Does that require making any changes to your behaviour? To your plans? To your relationships?

Who? **An unnamed foot soldier in the Amalekite army [Amale-what? The Amalekites were the nomadic descendants of Amalek, Esau's grandson; skilled in guerrilla warfare and very brutal, they were the constant torment of Israel.]**

When? **Around 1000 BC**

Why? **Hustling for position or advantage can be very foolish**

Where? **2 Samuel 1**

The Amalekite soldier

This story opens with two kings doing battle with two different enemies of Israel. On the one hand you have King Saul. On the other you have King David, who had been secretly anointed as Saul's successor by Samuel, but it wasn't yet public knowledge.

One battle is in the north of the country, on Mount Gilboa; the other takes place far south at a place called Ziklag.

In the first battle, Saul and the Israelite army suffer a massive defeat at the hands of the Philistines, resulting in the death of Saul and his three sons. It's a wipeout and Saul doesn't die well. Mortally wounded, he fails to get a man to finish him off and so he throws himself on his sword.

In the second battle, David launches a highly successful raid on the Amalekites. Ziglag was David's city. It had been given to him by Achish, the king of Gath, but raiders were destroying it and had taken away the wives and children of David and his soldiers. Now remember, this is David we are talking about. As a warrior with a habit of leaving no one alive after a battle (including women and children, see 1 Samuel 27:9), there was no way he was going to let his city be destroyed by the Amalekites.

2 Samuel begins with a two-day rest and a lull in the fighting for David and his men. It's then that we meet the man of the moment. Stumbling into the camp,

covered in dust and grime, clothing torn, the Amalekite soldier brings word of Saul's demise.

An interrogation begins. David is a master interrogator. He probes for details.

The thing is, we know the true version of events. Saul took his own life. So what on earth was this guy doing?

He was lobbying for position.

There are some giveaways:

- He just 'happened to be on Mount Gilboa' (verse 6). Oh, really? You mean to say you were the sole survivor of a mass slaughter? You just happened to be in the midst of all the chariots and horses and fighting – and lived?
- He appears to have lifted Saul's stuff – his crown and the band from his arm (verse 10) – after perpetrating the final fatal blow to the king's body. David's suspicions are aroused. Maybe he's a scavenger come from looting the battlefield bodies?
- He doesn't answer the question when asked how he knows that Saul's son Jonathan is also dead. Missing out detail is a sure sign that you are making stuff up… especially in response to a direct question.
- He calls David 'my lord' and yet he is an Amalekite (verse 10). As a potential kingmaker – the man who lays the crown at the feet of the next king – this man has his own future in mind!

He looked for promotion and advantage. What he got was death.

David, full of anger and grief that the soldier should lift his hand against the Lord's anointed, has him struck down.

We can learn some important lessons from the Amalekite soldier and wider issues of honour and the Lord's anointing:

- You reap what you sow. It's a strong biblical principle. Check out Galatians 6:7; Proverbs 11:18 and 22:8.
- Deal in lies and untruth and it will be your undoing. Maybe not as swiftly as it

was for this guy, but the truth will come out and you will have to deal with the consequences. Not good.

- David killed the Amalekite not because of his lies, nor because he took Saul's belongings. He struck him down because he touched the Lord's anointed. Once a king was anointed by God, only God had the right to touch or remove him. Even though Saul had gone rotten by this time, still the anointing of God was on him.

Don't push this last point too far but consider this: people tend to develop cultures of complaining. Most groups of people end up moaning about something or someone when they get together. Typically, we moan about those in authority, be it bosses at work or pastors at church. I think these verses give us a clear indication that those whom God has set in authority over us are his to deal with. Let's make sure we honour those God has appointed to lead us.

QUESTIONS

- Are you guilty of lobbying for position which might be compromising your behaviour as a believer?
- Do you complain and criticise the Lord's anointed?

ACTIONS

- Determine to be truthful on all occasions, even if it is going to be painful!
- Honour and respect those in authority.
- Find something positive to say about your boss and/or your pastor to your colleagues/church friends.
- Repent of any activity that cuts across the above!

18

Who? **King of Israel, red-blooded man of passion**
When? **Around 1000 BC**
Why? **He had to deal with all the stuff men have to deal with... and finished well**
Where? **His story opens in 1 Samuel 16 and runs through to the opening of 1 Kings**

David was an alpha male.

He came to prominence by taking down Goliath on the battlefields. Cutting off his head and holding it high in front of the enemy hordes of panicking Philistines, he showed that his courage and his heart for God were bigger than his teenage frame and penchant for poetry suggested.

He was a leader of leaders. While serving as an officer in King Saul's army he gained a fearsome reputation as a brutal killer of thousands and a gifted military strategist. He became a revered hero of the people.

When the people started the chant of 'Saul has killed his thousands but David his tens of thousands', it didn't exactly help the tense relationship between Saul and David. Saul got so eaten up by jealousy that he tried to kill David more than once. Some insecurity!

Eventually David was forced to hide in the desert. Against all the odds and assisted by a ragtag gang of guys reminiscent of the *A Team*, he eventually wiped out the marauding Amalekites and became King of Judah (the southern kingdom). Then, after taking out Ishbosheth – son of Saul and ruler of Israel – David became king of a newly united kingdom, ruling from 1005 BC to 965 BC.

David was a killer, poet, harpist, swordsman, statesman, inspirational general and serial lover.

Life and passion flowed through his veins and adrenalin was his life force.

He fought alongside three warrior brothers, all of whom had superhuman abilities to wage war. There was Jashobeam, who once killed 800 enemy warriors in one battle. Then there was Eleazar, the warrior who stood alone beside David killing Philistines with his sword in such numbers that he only stopped when he could no longer lift his sword. Finally there was Shammah, who wasn't against taking on a whole field of enemies all by himself.

David was their leader and their brother. At one point, talking about the men closest to him, David refused to drink water, even though he was dehydrated, to illustrate that the water was to him as precious as the blood of his fellow warriors. He was a giant among men and as fiercely godly as he was fiercely violent.

And then he got derailed:

- Not by a beautiful woman in a miniskirt.
- Not even by going where he shouldn't have gone.
- He was derailed by his **heart**.

Let me explain...

David probably already knew Bathsheba. Her husband Uriah was one of David's elite men, part of the band of brothers who was able to walk freely past the personal bodyguard and speak face to face with David.

Uriah was not in the inner circle of 'the three' but he was close. He was used to David asking him for military opinions and was probably as comfortable in the king's presence for a chat as fighting by his side on the battlefield. He was loyal unto death.

Shame the king wasn't.

We can assume that David knew Uriah's wife, Bathsheba. In fact, it's obvious that she lived near the palace. Near enough to be seen quite clearly by David when he took his **stroll**.

Maybe David had taken a **stroll** at various times in the past. Perhaps he got to know when she would be taking her purification bath. Perhaps he had taken a wrong turning in his mind months before.

Yes, this is all speculation – but it seems quite possible to me.

David had no hesitation in sending his guards to fetch her with the sole purpose of having sex with her. And he had no hesitation, on finding out that she was pregnant, in hatching a cover-up plan that was ruthless and cold and meant the death of his loyal brother warrior. He even sent a gift to Uriah before plotting his death. Refusing to drink water to demonstrate love for his brother warriors sounds a bit lame now, doesn't it?

I want to go a stage further.

Bathsheba had just had her period. That's why she was bathing – in accordance with the customs as described in Leviticus 15:19–24 and 2 Samuel 11:4. In other words, David actually slept with her when it was pretty much safe to go for it without much danger of pregnancy. David was trying to find a safe time to sin. With God there is no such thing. Sin sexually and repetitively without dealing with it and it will come out.

Well, Bathsheba did get pregnant and their son died as a direct result of David's adultery. His kingdom was never the same again. His family was ripped apart by heartache, rape and murder. He saw his sons get killed and the nation who once loved him turn against him in rebellion. Even his own son Absalom turned on him, going head to head in battle. Absalom, who should have been David's successor, inherited all the worst traits of his father as well as some of the good ones. But, instead of repenting like David, he just went from bad to worse and ended up being stabbed to death by his father's soldiers.

Sin has harsh consequences.

I don't want to finish there because thankfully David didn't end badly. He had to learn the hard way to deal with his dark centre. But David finished well. He repented, got past the turmoil and led the people as well as he could. He is remembered in the Hebrews 11 'hall of fame' and was even quoted by Jesus.

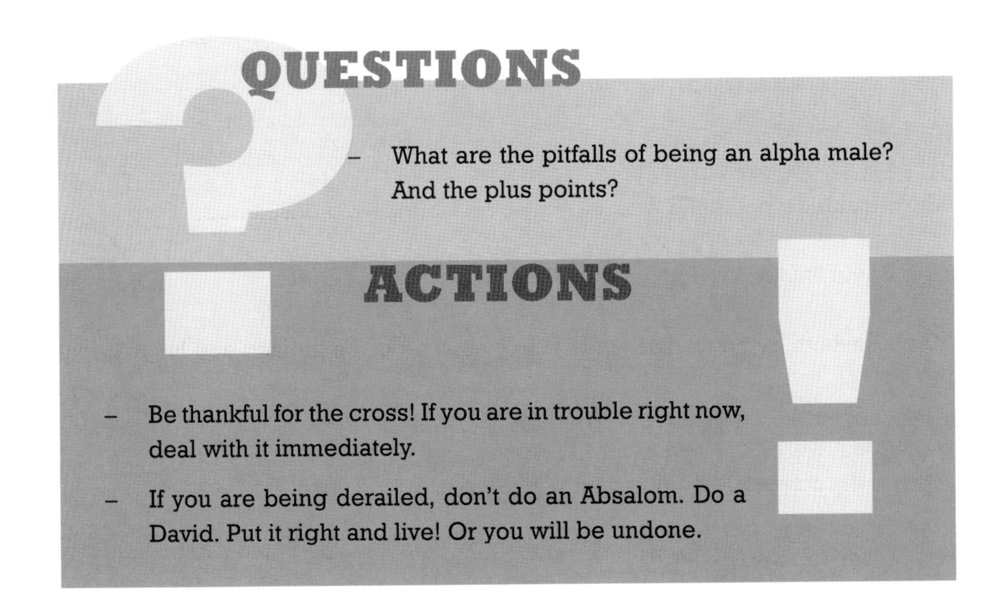

QUESTIONS

- What are the pitfalls of being an alpha male? And the plus points?

ACTIONS

- Be thankful for the cross! If you are in trouble right now, deal with it immediately.
- If you are being derailed, don't do an Absalom. Do a David. Put it right and live! Or you will be undone.

Who? **Saul's disabled grandson and son of Jonathan, David's closest friend**
When? **Somewhere around 1000 BC**
Why? **One of the most heart-warming stories in the Bible, with plenty to teach us**
Where? **2 Samuel 9**

Mephibosheth

In David's day, once you had defeated an enemy, you wiped everyone and everything out. You removed all physical traces of the enemy in order to leave things as if they had never existed. This especially applied to those who might present a challenge to your authority at a later date.

Mephibosheth (a real challenge to both my spelling and pronunciation skills) was a relative of King Saul. Potentially someone for an enemy faction to gather around. So, in the culture of the time, his life was in very real danger.

He was also crippled in both legs. In those days, if you had a disability your prospects were grim. In ancient Egypt it was common practice to leave a person with a disability out in the wilderness to die, or to have them stoned.

King David was different.

Mephibosheth dined as one of the king's sons all of his life and had his material needs met. Unbelievable! And it set an example to the whole nation.

Mephibosheth would have counted himself as worthy as a dead dog. A loser. Fit only for the scrap heap. He had zero self-esteem.

David believed him to be a fellow human being worthy of dignity and honour. Is this the first example of a declaration of rights for the disabled?

David looked to the heart of the man because he was a man of the heart and not outward appearance. As a youth he had stunned the armies of Saul by taking on the massive Goliath. Maybe he always remembered how people looked down on him before he fought Goliath, calling him 'only a boy'. And he determined to see people for what and who they really were.

I'll tread carefully here, but I'm pretty sure that men all too readily categorise other men. They are quick to view some as less able than them – and I'm not just talking physically.

Have you noticed the way men behave when they get together in a group? We scratch and sniff around each other, all working out our relative positions in the hierarchy. God's men don't look at others like that. We see each man as equal and consider others better than ourselves.

David's treatment of Mephibosheth sets us an example which underlines that every man has intrinsic value before God. I feel sure that for the rest of his life he held his head high. That's some gift from David; and an act of grace we would do well to emulate.

QUESTIONS

- Who do you know that can be given dignity by your acceptance and affirmation?

ACTIONS

- Remember – in your heart and actions as well as your head – that no human being is of lesser value than any other.
- Plan to spend time with a man who is struggling with or has overcome a disability. Ask what life is like from his perspective. Make any necessary adjustments to your thinking and living in the light of that knowledge.

20

Who? Prophet full of guts; a mover and shaker in the background
When? At the time of King David
Why? Because of his sheer courage
Where? 2 Samuel 12

NATHAN

Nathan's story is intriguing. He doesn't get many column inches, but when he appears he has a massive impact. It's a bit like keeping your star player on the bench until the last few minutes and then watching him run the legs off everyone. Just as one focused player in a football game can make all the difference, so can a real man of God.

Another thing: Nathan was not only in the premier league because he was gifted. He was also one gutsy player.

I believe men are required to have courage. I expect there were many times in Nathan's life when he had to overcome fear. Courage is not the absence of fear; it's the mastery of it.

Benjamin Franklin said this: '**A man without courage is like a knife without an edge.**' Well, Nathan had an edge and had to walk on it... many times!

Nathan worked with King David. He was a prophet – a man used by God to convey messages to nations or individuals. Prophets had a tough job because not every message was a congratulatory one! Sometimes prophets had to bring warnings, or messages of God's judgement and anger. Put bluntly, it wasn't a job for the faint-hearted or insecure.

Nathan was a good candidate for the job. His first recorded outing was a good one. You can read it in 2 Samuel 7 or 1 Chronicles 17. He was sent to King David to tell him that he would have a name and a kingdom that would last for ever. That was the easy bit. The true test of character is seen when we have to deal in bad news... and Nathan's time would soon come!

NATHAN

David was an awesome man and a fierce warrior. To have to confront such a man with a tough message was not an easy job. But Nathan was the man sent to King David after lust had got the better of him. Guilty of murder and adultery, David was in denial. And Nathan was the man to shake him out of it. It wasn't an easy confrontation and could have gone very badly indeed.

Many times in both my career in finance and my church ministry I've had to have confrontational meetings. They are never easy. Most times my heart would be beating fast. We can only guess how Nathan felt when God told him what he had to do. The message he had to take was that God was more than a tad displeased with David. Nathan also had to tell him that God was going to take the life of the son born to him and Bathsheba.

Nathan didn't come in from the cold to talk to David. He was a colleague, often by his side as a friend, mentor and guide. But after going through with delivering such a devastating message, you might think that the relationship between Nathan and David would be over. Not a bit of it. It seems that Nathan stayed close to David. It's possible that he wrote the books we call Chronicles for David. He had a role in protecting David when Adonijah tried to take David's power at the end of his life. We also know that Nathan had a hand in the organisation of temple worship.

Sometimes, just as Nathan did, you've just got to tell it as it is to the people you are close to.

Sometimes God might put something on your heart to say to another man that's not easy to say. If you are a true friend, you will say it. Not out of spite, not with a judging heart, but out of genuine concern.

I guess David could have put Nathan to death if he had wanted. Certainly he could have made Nathan disappear. However, he didn't! That was a hallmark of David's maturity and willingness to take bad news on the chin. And it shows his respect for Nathan.

I always rate a man highly who tells me the truth because I really need to hear it. All too often men can't divide personal from professional. That's not a good way to be. Robust working relationships mean that you tell it as it is (always keeping in mind how you want to be spoken to) and don't carry it over into your personal friendship. That way we mature.

QUESTIONS

- What was the source of Nathan's courage?
- Can you think how you might need Nathan's courage in your work situation? At home? At church?
- Are you able to speak honestly and still be full of grace?

ACTIONS

- Don't let the fear of man stop you from saying what is right and true.
- Be prepared to say things that won't win you popularity contests.
- Don't let the failings of friends or colleagues determine the rest of your relationships with them.

21

Solomon

Who? **Second son of David and Bathsheba, King of Israel for 40 years, wise, rich and into construction in a big way**
When? **About 970 BC**
Why? **Even the wisest can lose the plot**
Where? **The first 11 chapters of 1 Kings are his story and Proverbs is a collection of his wise sayings**

Let's cut to the chase. At his peak, Solomon had:

- 700 wives; and the Bible says he loved them all! (1 Kings 11:1)
- 300 concubines
- written 3000 proverbs
- composed 1005 songs
- built the temple
- rebuilt a few cities
- established military bases
- redefined the tribal boundaries of Israel...

Not bad going really.

David gave Solomon a profound and remarkable charge that's really worth reading. You can find it in 1 Kings 2:2–4.

For a time Solomon ran with it. The depth of his wisdom and teaching is still hailed to this day. Even among people who don't know much about the Bible he is remembered for the story of how he handled a dispute of two women fighting over a baby. It's even been in a movie! If you don't know the story, check it out in 1 Kings 3.

Then everything went pear-shaped. Yet another great man was derailed by his attraction to beautiful women.

Having been told not to intermarry with those outside of Israel (1 Kings 11:2,3) Solomon caved in to lust and desire. Like many men before him and since, he couldn't say no. Once he had opened himself up to lust, the dam burst and flooded his spirit with desire. Slowly over time it corrupted him, blunted his edge and blurred his focus. 1 Kings 11:4 sums it all up and makes for sad reading: '… his heart was not fully devoted to the LORD his God… '

I mean, what on earth was he thinking? He even had altars set up to the likes of Chemosh, a god who required child sacrifice. Don't soften it up. It meant children were often burned alive or had their skulls broken and were left to die.

Understandably God became angry with Solomon. After his death everything he had built was slowly undone and the kingdom of Israel started to split up. In fact God said he would tear it away from Solomon and that's just what happened.

In summary, Solomon messed up.

Being a man of God is about the heart. Taking a wrong turning is one thing; not doing anything about it is another. I don't suppose Solomon woke up one day and decided out of the blue to set up altars to other gods. I think his decline happened over time as a result of an ongoing drip drip of disobedience.

Just think of all those proverbs he wrote and all the wisdom they represent. And still he lost the plot. It's a salutary lesson. No matter how strong in God you were in your heyday, staying the course is what counts.

QUESTIONS

- Read again the charge given to Solomon by his father. Is it something you could live by?

ACTIONS

- Make sure there are people around you who are welcome to speak into your life, so that you don't take a gradual wrong turning.

22

Who? **A prophet who led an amazing life**
When? **About 850 to 800 BC**
Why? **A picture of what it means to run after God**
Where? **1 Kings 19:19–21, then 2 Kings 2–8**

Elisha

When Elisha left the oxen he was tending and ran after his new mentor Elijah, we get an insight into his passion for God. Not many of us run after anything – except maybe a banknote if it blows down the street.

Elisha recognised something worth running after and dropped everything. He was to be running after God constantly for the rest of his life.

Whether it was making an iron axe float (2 Kings 6:5–7), turning poison into food (2 Kings 4:38–41), raising the dead (2 Kings 4:8–37) or blinding whole armies (2 Kings 6:8 – 7:20) he never stopped pursuing God and reaching incredible levels of faith that are hard for us to grapple with.

The distinctive thing about Elisha was that while he walked among kings and rulers he was also a man of the people. He shunned palaces, preferring to stay with 'normal' people. One time, for example, he stayed in the home of a widow and blessed her with a supply of oil that saved her kids from slavery. Another time it was with a barren woman and her husband, who then had a child as a gift from God.

It seems likely he never forgot his roots as an ordinary working man. So many men get to high positions and forget where they came from.

He could be tender – crying over his nation and blessing the poor – but Elisha could also show a hard edge.

One particular incident would be humorous if it wasn't for the pretty poor outcome for those on the receiving end. One time, as he was walking along the road, a group of kids started on him – taking the mickey out of his lack of hair, calling him 'Baldy'. Three thousand years ago – and teenagers were being teenagers back then! Well, Elisha does more than give them an ASBO. He calls down a curse from God and 42 of them get mauled by a couple of wild bears (2 Kings 2:23,24).

What's that all about? Did he have a short fuse? Insecurity about his baldness?

I think in reality it's neither of those things. The bottom line is that a prophet was God's representative and therefore a holy man. Not a man to ridicule or threaten. On the other hand, if you looked after Elisha and showed him respect you got blessed – for example, the widow and the oil or the barren woman and her healing. But dishonour him and expect to get it in the neck – literally!

No, he was no soft touch. Far from woolly and cuddly. These days we dress spirituality in a fluffy cloud of snugly cosiness. Elisha demonstrates a robust and gritty prophetic edge we would do well to learn from. Believers aren't called to be like sickly sweet icing sugar but more like gritty sharp salt, retarding decay and stopping the rot.

There's no doubt that Elisha carried a unique anointing from God. Perhaps this was best illustrated when a dead man was thrown into Elisha's grave. When the corpse touched Elisha's bones, the man was raised to life (2 Kings 13:21). There was something truly dynamic about him so that even in death the power of God rested on him.

QUESTIONS

- What do you make of the 42 youths mauled by the bear?
- What's the evidence for humility in Elisha's life?

ACTIONS

- Don't be sugar; be salt.
- Give respect to the men of God that you know.

23

Who? **King of Judah**
When? **About 700 BC**
Why? **Because we're all prone to having the odd blind spot!**
Where? **2 Kings 18–20**

Hezekiah

This man was a hero. He has a great obituary: Hezekiah 'did what was right in the eyes of the LORD ... Hezekiah trusted in the LORD, the God of Israel ... There was no one like him ... He held fast to the LORD and did not cease to follow him; he kept the commands the LORD had given Moses' (2 Kings 18:3,5,6).

Not a bad thing to be said about you, is it?

I wonder what they'll say about me.

'Carl Beech ... he loved pasties... '

Whether it was smashing up idols, restoring worship in the temple, praying before taking action or cutting down idols, Hezekiah was your man. Several times he faced a crisis and in every situation he turned to God first before trying to fix things with his own action plan.

The superpower threat at that time came from Assyria. There was something akin to a cold war going on, sort of a Cuban missile crisis without Cuba and the missiles. Assyria – led by a certain Sennacherib, a bad guy with muscle who wasn't afraid to use it – wanted the area called Judah but Hezekiah was going to have none of it. But first things first. Hezekiah didn't gather the troops. Nor did he strengthen the walls. Or form a Dad's Army of volunteer soldiers. Not at first anyway. The first thing he did was **pray** and get the people right with God. Now that's a good tip. When the chips are down and your back's against the wall, what do **you** do? Panic? Try to fix it? Or turn to God?

So far so good for Hezekiah. He turns to God and then worries about getting things sorted on a human level. And guess what? God spares him. In fact, not only that but Sennacherib dies at the hands of his own sons – as prophesied by Isaiah, who's also around at this time.

Later in his life, Hezekiah nearly dies. Instead of going to the doctor, he prays. And guess what? God heals him and he's promised another 15 years of life.

There are repeated lessons here. God first… physical response second.

So powerful was the witness of Hezekiah's faith that word spread about him and even the mighty Babylonians chose to leave him alone. Put in context, that's a bit like the United States of America being nervous of attacking Portugal!

Pretty good stuff, right?

However… and this is a big HOWEVER…

All of us have an Achilles heel. That's just the way it is. All of us have blind spots and weaknesses. Hezekiah was pretty much on top of his game spiritually – but he had one serious flaw. Check it out from 2 Kings 20:12–19. But hold onto your seats! Did you spot it? Can you believe it?

'I'm alright, Jack. As long as everything's OK in my lifetime then who cares what happens after I'm gone? Yeah, the nation might get destroyed and the people become slaves, but it's cool – because it won't happen till I'm gone!'

Err, hello? Houston calling! Did we hear that correctly? Can't believe it, can you?

I'm convinced that many of our problems in church and, indeed, in day to day life, come from the same attitude – 'As long as we're happy, then let's not worry about the next generation…'

That's such a **bad** attitude.

For Hezekiah, this really is a sad moment in a great life.

Do not live just for yourself and for your own comfort and happiness! Think of those who will come after you. I can promise you that when you do that, life will go well in the present anyway, because you have moved from selfishness to selflessness!

This applies to both business and church. The greatest leaders look to the future and don't just concentrate on themselves. They imagine something far greater and better for future generations than they were ever involved in. They are simply content to have once been a part of it. Is that how you are at work? Is that how you are at church?

Peace in our time? Nah! Let's do battle so that we can give those that follow us a blessing!

QUESTIONS

- It's hard to see our own blind spots. Is there someone close to you who you can ask about yours?
- How are you leaving any kind of legacy for those that come after you?

ACTIONS

- Take time to think and pray for the next generation – in your family and in your church. What are their needs? What battles could you fight today that would bless them tomorrow?

24

Who? Governor of Jerusalem, a CEO who rolled up his sleeves
When? Around 445 BC
Why? Amazing leader and strategist
Where? He has a whole Old Testament book named after him

Nehemiah

Nehemiah is awesome! Contained within this all-too-often-overlooked story is some really pithy stuff that has the lessons you need to see you function with greater impact at home, work and church.

So here goes...

Nehemiah is in a place called Susa. Word comes to him that the walls of Jerusalem have been broken down. It's then we get the first insight into the heart of the man. The first thing he does isn't to dash off and draw up an action plan – as most men would. He gets on his knees and prays, fasts and mourns. Not for the lunch hour or even for 24 hours... but for days!

Only then does he go to King Artaxerxes and plead with him for safe passage back to Jerusalem to scan the damage to the walls of his beloved city.

Lesson 1: Precede your activity with loads of prayer and fasting (giving up food for a spiritual reason, and to spend extra time with God) especially when you are up against it. It's a key to success.

Artaxerxes provides safe passage and Nehemiah goes to inspect the walls. The news isn't good. Just thinking about reconstructing such a massive wall out of huge stones would have been morale-crushing for most men. But not for Nehemiah!

Lesson 2: Do some research and think positively!

The key is in 2:20! Check it out. Nehemiah knows the secret of his success in this venture isn't just about good planning. It's about being in the presence of God! Above all else, it was God who would grant success.

Lesson 3: Remember where your strength comes from!

And so the rebuilding starts (chapter 3). Even the priests get their hands dirty and the perfume-makers start making cement. Everyone gets stuck in to the action and grafts hard. Whole families are involved, with daughters working alongside fathers and even regional rulers abandoning their position of high office to get busy.

Lesson 4: Don't ever think your high position precludes you from getting stuck in on the factory floor when the need arises!

By chapter 4 the opposition is starting to make its presence felt. But, facing ridicule and threats, the people don't cave in. They work even harder – 'with all their heart'. No name calling is going to stop these guys.

Lesson 5: Sticks and stones may break my bones – but I'll just ignore the ridicule!

So the real grind begins. With swords in one hand and trowels in the other, and in a constant state of high alert, the people crack on. They stand guard day and night, with a constant flow of prayer. They even have to labour one-handed, with a weapon in the other hand and swords strapped to their sides.

Lesson 6: Pray **and** take action!

Nehemiah knows that prayer is important – but he also needs to take action! God could strike down his enemies, but he's also prepared for a fight if necessary.

By chapter 5 the internal tension was creeping in. Faced with extreme hardship, the rich are exploiting the poor. Nehemiah is a genuinely caring manager and doesn't ignore the cry of the people. Even with all the other pressures, he takes time to listen to the needs of his team. He instinctively knows that their concerns are important and he genuinely cares. And so he deals with the problem head-on.

Lesson 7: Don't get so wrapped up in your work that you forget the people who are standing with you and working alongside you.

All too often we use people as commodities to get a job done. That's not right! People are much more than commodities. Nehemiah is a leader who understands this.

By chapter 6 the wall is rebuilt in an absolutely astonishing and miraculous 52 days. The result is that those who oppose the rebuilding lose confidence because it becomes clear whose side God is on. Awesome!

And so there you have the main thrust of it. There is much more we could say. For instance, we could talk about the fact that the first thing the Israelites do is dedicate the work to God rather than pat themselves on the back. We could talk about the power of God; or the incredible social reforms that Nehemiah enacted.

However, for now, note this: To achieve profound breakthrough we need two things working in harmony. Prayer and action. One without the other adds up to a flawed strategy. Some people say, 'If only we prayed more!' Still others say, 'If only we got off our backsides more!' The truth is, we need both!

Nehemiah was the CEO who rolled up his sleeves. He probably took the skin off his hands. Now that's leadership!

QUESTIONS

- How are prayer and action working together in your life?
- If you're successful, do you think about where your strength comes from?
- If you're not successful, do you know who to turn to?

ACTIONS

- Examine your life at work, home and church and think about what Nehemiah can teach you in each of those spheres.

Who? A disempowered slave who honoured God
When? About 605–530 BC
Why? Daniel was all about zero compromise
Where? He's another guy with a whole book named after him

Daniel

Daniel's story is not for the faint-hearted.

He was in Judah when Nebuchadnezzar the King of Babylon besieged the city, thoroughly defeated the Israelites and carried Daniel off with a number of other guys to face a lifetime of captivity. Not a good start in life for a young man looking to make his way in the world.

We know that Daniel was connected to the nobility, good-looking, bright and fit.

The orders from Nebuchadnezzar were clear. Daniel, along with three other young men called Hananiah, Mishael and Azariah (more famously known as Shadrach, Meshach and Abednego), were to be indoctrinated into the Babylonian way of doing things, taught their literature and culture, and then enter the king's service.

It didn't end there. It's quite possible that as part of their captivity they were castrated as well. All those who served as court officials were eunuchs, and as Daniel and co were to be educated and overseen by the chief eunuch, it's quite likely that they had to join their ranks.

If you have any insight into the methods of castration employed at that time, you'll be wincing by now!

Daniel decided very quickly where he would draw the line. He might be castrated, he might be in captivity, he might be forced into the service of an ungodly king – but he decided to hold the line when it came to personal integrity. He might have to live and serve in enemy territory but there was no way he was going to compromise his godly values.

The parallels for us are startling. We live in enemy territory and are under pressure to compromise all the time. Question is, do we hold the line? Do we dare to be like Daniel?

He chose his first battle straight away. He was offered top quality nosh and decent wine from the king's own table. But Daniel knew that it would have been offered to idols. So he refused it. Even the guards were worried. If it all went pear-shaped, it would be their heads on the block.

But God honoured him and after ten days on a diet of vegetables and water, Daniel and his three companions looked fitter and better than anyone else (Daniel 1:11–15).

Point made.

God honours those who honour him.

Think about that next time you laugh at a filthy joke the boss tells, just to keep 'in' with him.

Later, under another king called Darius, officials jealous of his high standing (he was now a top official in the land and due to be promoted to be number one over the whole kingdom) could find no corruption or flaw in Daniel's work, so they tried to stitch him up. They got an edict passed banning worship of any god other than the king.

Daniel was going to have none of it. In fact he got right in their faces. As soon as he heard about the edict he went home, opened the window that faced Jerusalem and prayed on his knees three times a day.

As a result of that bit of 'line holding' he got thrown to the lions... very hungry, underfed lions. You know the rest if you went to Sunday School. The lions refused to eat until the corrupt officials got thrown in there, when the lions suddenly rediscovered their appetites.

Think about that next time you feel a bit worried about mentioning to people that you go to church, let alone that you are someone who follows Jesus.

If ever we needed a role model for a bit of guts and moral integrity, we have one in Daniel.

He served under different kings and never once compromised. Never once did he let up, dilute his beliefs, or back down. He put his worship of God before his career and God honoured every step of the way.

Perhaps a key insight is found when we look at Daniel's friends who were captured with him. Before being thrown into a fiery furnace they basically said this, 'We may live, we may die. God might save us, he might not. Whatever he chooses to do, he is good, and we won't budge!' (Daniel 3:13–28).

In other words: win, lose or draw, God is God and he is good.

And that's what set these guys apart. They didn't expect it all to be rosy but they knew God could be trusted no matter what.

What about you at work?

Have you defined the line that you won't cross? Do you put career advancement before integrity? Or the desire to honour God before your career?

The thing is this: we need believers in every sphere of life, from the forces to pharmaceuticals, from sales to anything else that starts with 's'. We can and should work in difficult areas that cause us to ask difficult questions and face moral dilemmas. If we aren't doing that, perhaps life is too cosy. The secret is knowing when to hold the line, and then having the guts to trust God with your livelihood and maybe, one day, your life.

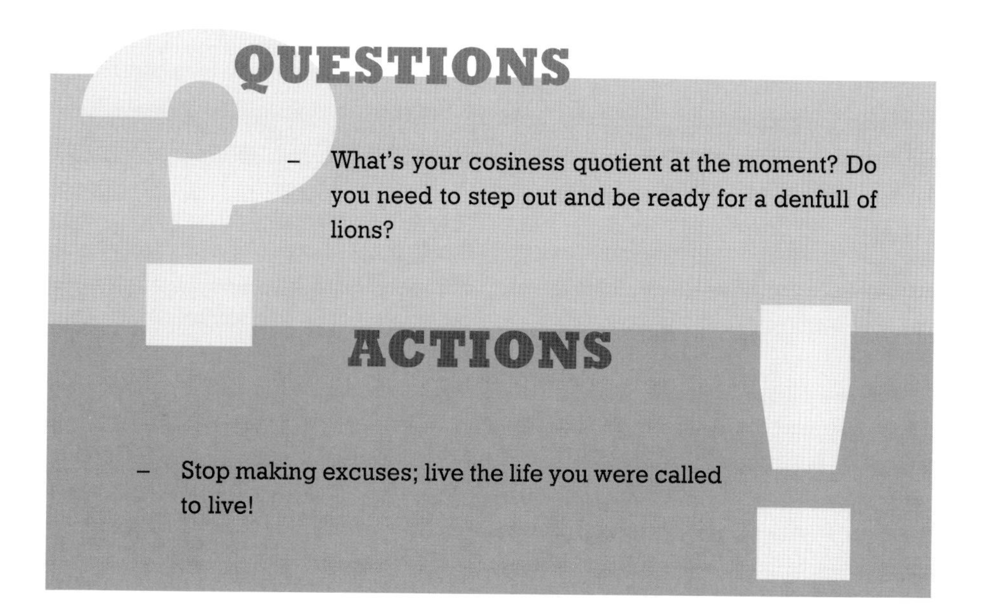

QUESTIONS

- What's your cosiness quotient at the moment? Do you need to step out and be ready for a denfull of lions?

ACTIONS

- Stop making excuses; live the life you were called to live!

26

Who? A talented guy who got delusional
When? Around 600 BC
Why? A masterclass in pride
Where? The first four chapters of Daniel

Nebuchadnezzar

Pride crops up more than a few times in this book – mainly because it crops up a lot in men's lives and therefore appears loads in characters in the Bible.

You will see a constant theme emerge: Men who have pride get taken down more than a peg or two!

Nebuchadnezzar was an amazing man of huge power and influence. He built Babylon into the largest city of its time, covering maybe just under 3000 acres. His buildings were without compare. In fact, he was responsible for one of the ancient seven wonders of the world, the hanging gardens of Babylon, supposedly built to ease his wife's longing for the mountain springs of her homeland. Extravagant, eh? Be thankful when your wife only demands a trip to the mall!

On a military level Nebuchadnezzar was also awesome and was responsible for the invasion and conquest of Judah. I'm not going to go into massive detail about him, except to highlight a very key point.

One day he was having a stroll around his palace and surveying all that he had built, much in the manner that most men do when they have finished some DIY task. The difference on this occasion was that it was while patting himself on the back that he was struck down for his pride.

God had already warned him through a dream (and an interpretation of it by Daniel) that judgement was coming if he didn't sort himself out. He chose not to listen. We don't know why he didn't take heed. Probably just his pride.

I once read somewhere that Churchill, asked on his deathbed if he was ready to meet God, replied that he hoped God was ready to meet him. Great and talented people often suffer delusion! But Nebuchadnezzar was about to have the 'messiah complex' knocked right out of him.

For seven years he lost his mind. Wandering as a madman, with the outward appearance of a messed up half-man, half-beast, he learned the hard way that actually it is God who gives and takes, builds and destroys. Not men.

At the end of the seven years, he knew who to give the credit to. He was never the same again. The mighty Nebuchadnezzar, feared ruler and conqueror, had been humbled.

QUESTIONS

- Run a check on your pride status. How are you doing? Do you know for sure the source of all you have and are?

ACTIONS

- Be very careful who you give the credit to for the good things you have.
- Keep yourself humble before God rather than have God teach you a lesson. Don't think he is beyond dealing with us in this life rather than the next... he loves us too much to leave us alone to mess up without correction.
- Offer up a prayer right now, thanking God for what he has given you, particularly if you have known some recent success. He really likes that!

27

Who? **A top-drawer prophet who literally lived out his message**
When? **Around the same time as Isaiah, 740–700 BC**
Why? **This is love!**
Where? **His short book is squeezed in somewhere near the end of the Old Testament, straight after Daniel.**

When we think about love we immediately conjure up romantic images of candlelit dinners, a beach in the moonlight or strolls in the countryside.

When the Bible talks about love, it tends to be just a little bit stronger!

Sometimes prophets were called on to live out lives that were symbolic. That was Hosea's task and it was a tough one. Let's work through what that meant.

1 Hosea was told by God to marry a prostitute. So he did, without complaint. The idea was to show the people of Israel that they had been unfaithful to God

2 Hosea and his wife Gomer had a son. Most of us who have children loved choosing their names. Well, it wasn't much fun for Hosea. He was given his son's name, Jezreel, by God. Jezreel was a valley where there had been a lot of fighting and a lot of lives lost. The idea was to show that the leaders of the northern kingdom were going to pay for all the bloodshed. It's like being told today that you have to call your child 'Helmand Province'.

3 Next, the couple had a daughter. She had to be named 'No Pity' to show Israel that, although Yahweh will have pity on the southern kingdom of Judah, he is about to wipe out the northern kingdom of Israel.

4 Next, a son was born to Gomer. We don't know if he was Hosea's child because his name was to be 'Not Mine'. The child bore this shameful name to show that the northern

kingdom would also be shamed, for its people would no longer be known as God's people.

5 Chapter 2 describes a divorce. This divorce is basically a description of God breaking his ties with Israel. You guessed it: Hosea divorces his wife because she keeps committing adultery and he uses it as a picture to preach about God and Israel. But, he declares, God will one day take Israel back and love her again.

6 OK, you guessed it again! In chapter 3 he takes Gomer back, despite all the pain she's given him. In fact, Hosea has to buy her back because she has ended up in slavery to pay off her debts. This is yet another picture to show that God will take Israel back – but at great cost.

7 After he has done this, Hosea takes time before he gets intimate again with Gomer to demonstrate that although God will take Israel back, it's going to take time for Israel to have a king again.

Talk about being put through it! To be a prophet was to be completely signed up to living God's way and doing God's work. It was no easy task and meant huge personal sacrifice.

The thing is this: when you keep yourself close to God you also start to experience God's huge heart and compassion for people. What could Hosea do but serve him?

QUESTIONS

- How would it be if we kept ourselves so close to God that we felt his pain for people? How differently would you behave? How differently would the Church be?

ACTIONS

- 'There is no divine attribute more wonderful than the patience of God' (Dr John Benton, quoted in an anthology from Evangelical Press called 'Sifted Silver'). Think about how to demonstrate the truth of that in your daily life.

28

Who? Long-suffering, faithful servant of God
When? Uncertain – no one really knows
Why? Worship God no matter what!
Where? Another guy who has his own Old Testament book, just in front of Psalms, but look especially at the first three and the last three chapters

Job

- How can there be a God when… ?
- Why believe in God when he allows… ?
- My gran/mum/sister/dad/best mate died horribly, so I can't believe that God…
- How can there be a God when there are tsunamis… ?

You have probably heard statements like these and many more besides. As soon as you declare yourself to be a Christian, you invite these sorts of comments. It goes with the territory.

Most men then either shut down, or try to enter into some kind of theological debate or marathon apology to persuade everyone that God is actually good despite tsunamis and cancer…

Theologian John Calvin said: 'The disciples of Christ must walk among thorns, and march to the cross amidst uninterrupted afflictions!'

Oh, great!

But it's true.

I once visited a guy called Robin in hospital when he was in a really bad way. I had rarely seen someone suffering as much as he was. It was profoundly moving.

In the midst of all the pain Robin just kept saying… 'Praise the Lord!' He never got angry with God. Nor did he question, preferring to trust that the Lord was there and in control and that there was always a purpose.

When a new student pastor joined our church, one of the first visits I told him to make was to Robin. I figured he would learn more from a cup of tea with him than from a month or two with me!

The bottom line is this: we were never promised an easy life.

When we look at Job, we see how to hold the line when everything's going worse than belly up.

Job was a highly respected man. He was wealthy (Job 1:3; 42:12). He mixed with the great and the good and was known as one of Israel's greatest ancestors (Ezekiel 14:14). He had it all.

And then, for a time, it was all taken away.

In my office I keep the poem 'If' by Rudyard Kipling on my wall. I love it. It really speaks to me as a man. Written in 1909, it conveys some deep truths and more than a few motivational one liners. Including: **If you can meet with Triumph and Disaster and treat those two impostors just the same…** And it finishes with the line… **And – which is more – you'll be a Man, my son!**

Get hold of it and live the words.

I think you learn most about a person's character not when everything is going well, but when their back's against the wall. How they respond to disaster and hard knocks will tell you what a man is like deep inside.

The same applies to a man's faith. How he responds to tough times will tell you how deep his faith is. I mean, it's easy to praise God after the annual bonus, isn't it? But what about when you face losing everything?

Rees Howells, whose biography was called *Rees Howells: Intercessor*, once said that you 'don't know how much faith you have until it is tested'. True enough!

Job is a deep and long book and we won't be able to go into it in vast detail. Read it and then read it again and absorb its lessons.

In brief: Satan takes everything from Job, including his children's lives. It was all part of Satan's attempt to show God that when the chips were down, even a faithful man like Job would turn against him.

Wrong!

So Satan attacks Job's health as well. In fact, he develops a horrific disease.

Still Job didn't blame God.

Eventually Job did cry out to God – not to blame him but to ask questions. So bad was his life at one point that Job even questioned why he was born! We can only imagine how much pain he was in, emotionally and physically. He experienced total loss with no apparent way back. The grief must have been utterly overwhelming, and it all happened brutally fast.

Then come the famous 'Job's Comforters'. We have all experienced these well meaning friends who come along just when you don't need them, in order to give you lots of 'good' advice and counsel.

One of them said it was all to do with Job's sin! Well, thanks, mate!

Another said it must all have been his kids' fault.

And so it goes on...

Have you ever experienced that? Something goes wrong and everyone tries to give you spiritual reasons for the disaster, usually pointing at your own uselessness? It's so comforting, isn't it!

Eventually they give up and shut up and it's then that God makes two points to Job:

- He points to creation and asks if he could have done a better job.
- God points out that he controls the world, again asking Job if he could do it any better.

You can guess the answers. Job says he can see that God has everything well under control.

God then gives Job's three 'friends' a bit of a telling off, including telling them that Job needs to pray for them!!

Finally, God gave Job more children and even more money than he had ever had before.

Bottom line: God is good – all the time and in every way.

Job comes across to me as a man of real character and grit. He could take the rough with the smooth. Despite being in utter pain and turmoil, he never hit out at God or rejected him. Sure, he cried out. Yes, he wondered what the heck was going on. But he never turned away.

QUESTIONS

- Why do we blame God when things don't work out for us?
- Why do we always want to provide answers for every situation, including spiritual causes and effects?

ACTIONS

- Learn lessons from Job's friends. Sometimes, when someone you know is going through it, the last thing you should be doing is giving trite answers. Sometimes the best thing to do is just to be there and say very little. Less is definitely more when you are up against it!
- Next time it all goes wrong at work, don't whinge and get angry with God. Just trust that he is good and in control.

29

Who? A mover and shaker with a tough message from God
When? Around 740–680 BC
Why? Having met God, he remained unshakeable in his calling
Where? A long book in the centre of the Bible. Chapter 6 is a crucial one but a lot of the rest is also huge

It's one thing to stand alone as a follower of Jesus at work. It's another thing to stand alone in a nation. That was Isaiah's calling and it was a tough one.

We need to get a handle on what was happening on the world stage to understand just how tough it was for him.

For most of Isaiah's life, Assyria was the superpower. To the east of Judah and just across the mighty Euphrates river, Babylon – another major player – was emerging as a force to be reckoned with. Elsewhere, according to Roman mythology, Romulus and Remus were getting on with building Rome; and the Greek powerhouse of Sparta (famous for the Spartan warriors and the stories of Troy and later the battle of Thermopylae etc) was just being built. This, then, was the era of the first superpowers, of epic battles and struggles for supremacy. It was a time when the northern kingdom of Israel was to be conquered by Assyria; and Judah was to be left standing alone as a remnant nation of God's people.

Great time to get a job as a prophet, eh! Just for reference: Micah, Amos and Hosea were other prophets of God who were all around at the same time. Isaiah's task was to speak for God in the melting pot of war, intrigue and power struggles that characterised the time.

At that point, the nation of Judah was one wealthy place. And, true to form, people forgot about God because they were more focused on having a good time and getting the latest stuff. The rich people got very rich indeed, but the poor sank further into complete misery. They had no food and no clothing (Isaiah 3:14,15; 32:9–15)... and God was getting angry about it.

Alcohol featured heavily in people's lives. (Ring any alarm bells?) Corruption was rampant and people used their positions to trample even more on the poor. Even the prophets were failing to do the job God had given them. Instead of speaking out and telling people how God felt, they preached – as can so often happen now – what the people wanted to hear.

Then Isaiah rode into town.

He was a mover and shaker, well connected to the royal court. He had influence. He understood economics and politics and was well versed in literature, religion and history.

However, he was more than an ancient world equivalent of Jeremy Paxman. Because Isaiah understood God's heartbeat. He wasn't concerned about popularity or acceptance. He didn't care for being well thought of and was not a man to sacrifice truth for the sake of having invites to the best parties.

His focus was truth and justice. He consistently spoke up for the poor, the badly treated, the starving, the marginalised, the widow and orphans. While the rich got richer and the fat got fatter, Isaiah stood by the underdog with a message of judgement and doom for those who didn't get things sorted out...

Things started to get hot – literally! – for Isaiah when, still a young man, he had a life changing encounter in the temple. You can read it in Isaiah 6. It's not for the delicate. Put simply, Isaiah met God.

We can go into church very casually these days, our minds full of all kinds of stuff like lunch, work, the car, money, avoiding someone else. Isaiah probably went to worship God with an attitude of awe and the hope of having a time of encounter. What he got was off the Richter scale!

I won't go into the details, because you can and should read it for yourself. But what I will say is this: when God turns up in power, as he did with Isaiah, it focuses your mind. Despite being a man of God, being exposed to God's pure holiness made Isaiah feel totally dirty on the inside.

Immediately the call comes and Isaiah, completely overwhelmed, agrees. But it's only after agreeing that God gives him the detail...

Isaiah was to go to people who would not listen; he would speak and teach, yet people would just grow deafer to his pleas. He was to keep going until the nation he loved was in ruins and the people exiled.

Some call!

Imagine being called to a church in the knowledge that every time you preached more people would leave. In fact, imagine being called to a church in the certain knowledge that your sermons are going to cause the church to fall into ruin!

Isaiah had to tell people that God hates their prayers (chapter 1). He told them that their hands were covered in blood and that they had been trampling over the temple. He spoke of the coming of Jesus, knowing that the people would kill him. He forecast a time when the world would be devastated... and all the time his heart was breaking because he knew no one was listening. That's a painful ministry and a barren spiritual experience.

Isaiah, though, put obedience to God above personal comfort, popularity and prosperity. Ultimately, he put obedience and an ethos of zero compromise above even his own life; on refusing to recant, King Manasseh had him sawn in half between two planks of wood.

Words cannot honour this man enough.

QUESTIONS

- How important is it to you to be popular?
- What expectations do you have for the time you spend in church?

ACTIONS

- Spend some time thinking about God's holiness. What would be an appropriate response for you?

30

Who? **A prophet who knew more than a bit about God's glory**
When? **Probably around 620 BC**
Why? **Because we need to know that God's with us and is mighty**
Where? **You guessed – he's got his own book, very close to the end of the Old Testament**

Habakkuk

This isn't going to be long. Partly because we don't know much about Habakkuk and partly because I only want to highlight one thing.

Grab a coffee and a Bible and read this whole book through. It will only take five minutes and it might just change the way you think about prayer for ever.

Habakkuk operated in a tough time. He lived when Judah (the southern kingdom) was under threat from Babylon. He might have even lived to see Jerusalem attacked by the Babylonians in 597 BC.

His writings are special because they are so personal. That's why I'm bringing him to your attention. You basically get the inside track on his relationship with God. His book gives you a uniquely personal insight into a conversation between God and one of his mighty anointed prophets.

He starts off confused because he just can't work God out. He can't understand why God allows injustice and destruction. He can't understand why God seemingly does nothing to evil people. Sound familiar?

Then something remarkable and awesome happens. It comes in chapter 3.

God reveals his glory to Habakkuk. As a result, you get one of the most amazing and startling descriptions of the splendour of our God in the whole of the Bible: 'His splendour was like the sunrise; rays flashed from his hand... ' (3:4).

The thing that makes these few sentences so awe-inspiring is that he writes as if he has actually seen it...

Regularly I sit down and put everything aside – my Bible, my notes, my own agendas. Most men find that tough because we want to do stuff. I understand that. But I ask God to be with me and to show me his presence. I focus all my thoughts on him and use some of the words from Habakkuk, which I have memorised, as my focus:

> 'The Sovereign LORD is my strength;
> he makes my feet like the feet of a deer,
> he enables me to go on the heights' (3:19).

That's where I draw my strength from... taking time to soak in God's presence.

When we experience the heights of his glory and then go out to 'do stuff', we do it with even greater drive and effectiveness.

QUESTIONS

- What is the source of your strength?
- Do you cry out to God about injustice, like Habakkuk did?

ACTIONS

- Decide to give some time to experiencing God. The first time I ever did this, I cried on my knees for half an hour at the sense of God's being with me in my living room. It changed me for ever. My confidence in God being with me all the time went up more than a few notches. Find a quiet place, focus on his glory, and you may just be surprised by what you experience...

31

Who? A prophet who was wild, focused and gritty
When? Around AD 30
Why? He was relentless in his pursuit of God's kingdom
Where? Matthew 3 and 14:1–12

John the Baptist

'There came a man who was sent from God; his name was John' (John 1:6).

And he dressed in clothes made from coarse camel hair and he ate locusts and honey.

He had a far from ordinary start in life.

John enters the Bible stage when he was a man in his late twenties. Living in the desert, either as a loner or possibly as part of an ultra-strict Jewish sect called the Essenes, he was wandering around proclaiming a message of **repentance**. Repentance means to do a lifestyle U-turn, away from doing stuff that displeases God.

It was a powerful message from a powerful guy who was basically preparing the way for Jesus to begin his ministry. As part of his message he was baptising people in the river Jordan, preaching that the kingdom of God was near.

Some people thought that **he** was the Messiah, the chosen one, John made it clear that he wasn't.

Perhaps the most amazing moment of his career came when Jesus asked John to baptise him! Jesus and John were actually related (although this doesn't mean that they hung out together). We know this because of what it says in Luke 1:36, that the two men's mothers were related. We just don't know how.

Whatever the connection, the moment of baptism was profound. It immediately preceded Jesus' testing time in the desert and public launch of his ministry. And in a very real way proclaimed the end of John's. Because a short time later, John found himself in prison. The reason was simple. As well as declaring good news, John had been exposing bad news. In this case, the bad news was that King Herod had married his brother's wife while his brother was still alive – an act against the Mosaic law. Herod was bad news all round and, according to Luke 3:19, John was vocal about other stuff he did as well.

From the moment of his arrest, John knew that time was short. He wanted to know if he could die a fulfilled man, so Matthew 11 records an amazing conversation. John sends his disciples to Jesus to ask if Jesus really was the Messiah.

He just needed to make sure.

One last time…

Jesus sent a message back: 'Go back and report to John what you hear and see: The blind receive sight, the lame walk, those who have leprosy are cured, the deaf hear, the dead are raised, and the good news is preached to the poor.'

That's all John needed to hear.

A short time later he lost his head.

Maybe some of Jesus' words were in his heart as the sword swung down: **'Blessed is the man who does not fall away on account of me.'**

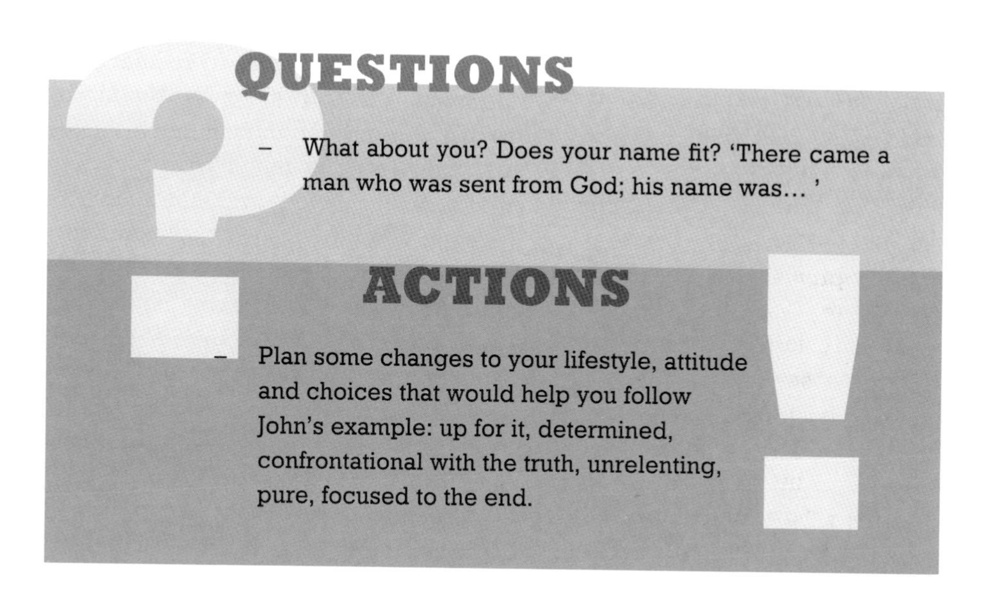

QUESTIONS

– What about you? Does your name fit? 'There came a man who was sent from God; his name was… '

ACTIONS

– Plan some changes to your lifestyle, attitude and choices that would help you follow John's example: up for it, determined, confrontational with the truth, unrelenting, pure, focused to the end.

32

Who? One tough character
When? In the time of Jesus
Why? Though he exercised huge power, he understood about authority
Where? Matthew 8:5–13

The centurion

The Roman army was the most feared and lethal instrument of war in the ancient world, characterised by discipline and commitment to the empire. Harsh, brutal practices in peacetime paid dividends in war, often with astonishing victories against the odds.

A centurion in the Roman army had huge power and awesome responsibility. Typically in charge of around 80 men (not 100, as you'd think), he routinely dealt out the beating called **castigatio**, otherwise known as being thumped by his wooden staff, and he could even execute a soldier for dereliction of duty.

Crucially, he was also a man **under** authority – and the same punishments that he meted out could be inflicted on him.

Anyone who wanted to be a centurion had to be at least 30 years of age and be recommended by others – usually men of higher rank. As he had probably joined up at 16, nearly half of his life would have been in the military. By this time, he was a war machine, totally dedicated to serving the emperor.

Such men paid the price. They were on a good salary with a good retirement scheme – if they lasted the required 20 years. Most didn't. They died in service. Death was pretty much inevitable.

So this is the man Jesus meets: hardened, tough, disciplined, world- and battle-weary, a man expecting to give his life to the empire. A man who recognised authority.

And that's what he saw in Jesus.

Authority.

In fact, there was a second centurion, who also understood about Jesus' authority. 'Surely he was the Son of God,' this centurion said at the cross (Matthew 27:54). He knew all about death. He had seen how men died under extreme pressure and in intense agony. He knew that Jesus died differently from other men.

These two centurions are men's men. Credible and down to earth. Not given to moments of weakness. Not ones to have the wool pulled over their eyes. And that's why Matthew uses their encounters ahead of the hundreds of other meetings that Jesus had.

But back to our first centurion! When he gave an order he was used to it being obeyed immediately. He knew that if Jesus gave a command for healing it would happen immediately. He recognised that Jesus worked for and with an even higher authority. He also knew that ultimately his own life was under the authority of Jesus.

QUESTIONS

- Are you a man whose life is under the authority of Jesus in every area?
- Are you a man who has faith that Jesus can and will do whatever he chooses to? Do you pray as if that were true? Do you live as if that were true?

ACTIONS

- Think about what lesson in submission you can learn from the centurion. By taking this on board, you may just find that your life of prayer and discipleship is hugely strengthened!
- Take Jesus seriously. Some of us guys can be a bit cynical about who Jesus is. This story gives us a bit of pointer that maybe he should be taken seriously after all. If a Roman centurion realises that he can't sit on the fence... what about you?

33

Who? Massively demonised man who got his life sorted – and then wouldn't shut up about it
When? In the days of Jesus
Why? Because sharing our stories with others can be challenging
Where? Mark 5:1–20

Legion

Legions were the Roman army equivalent of today's army regiments and could be up to 6000 men strong.

So when a host of demons announces its name as 'Legion', you know that means more than just a handful of demons are present. In fact, the poor man overtaken by them was in a complete mess. At one stage people had tried to chain him up because of his violent outbursts, but his demonic strength meant that the chains were as good as spaghetti. Worse than that, he was self-harming, naked, crying out in torment and in constant anxiety and stress.

Then he met Jesus.

It's a short and famous account. It will take you five minutes to read it.

But what of the man himself?

Totally healed, at peace and in his right mind, he just wanted to serve and follow Jesus and become part of the group of disciples.

But he was missing the point. Jesus knew that he would be far more effective telling his story in the town where he lived before he was taken over by demons. Jesus knew that the most powerful testimony to the goodness of God is a transformed life.

He knew that the man formerly known as Legion would never stay quiet.

The problem is that so many of us do stay quiet. Even those of us who have had dramatic encounters with God have a tendency to be rather shy about it.

Henry Ward Beecher, a prominent American preacher in the late 1800s, once said, 'If you want your neighbour to know what Christ will do for him, let your neighbour see what Christ has done for you... '

The man in this story became an overspill of passion for the kingdom because his life had been touched by the power of Jesus. And that's what witnessing is all about. It's an overspill.

I find it helpful to look back over the things that God has done for me on a regular basis. I find that the memories fuel my gratitude and therefore I talk more about what God has done. We so easily forget. I've known people who have experienced miracles, only to turn from God later.

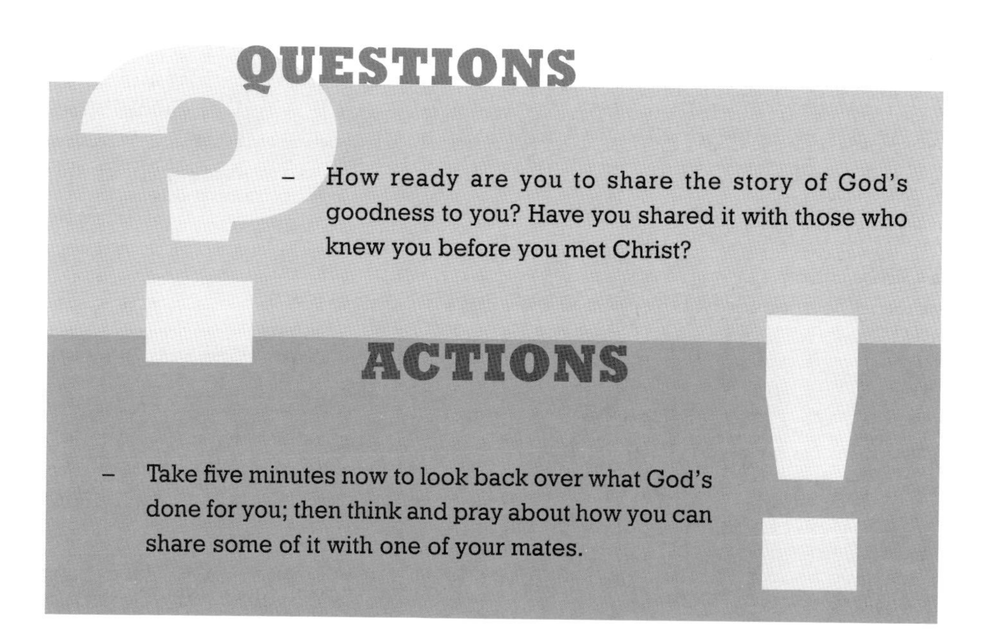

QUESTIONS

- How ready are you to share the story of God's goodness to you? Have you shared it with those who knew you before you met Christ?

ACTIONS

- Take five minutes now to look back over what God's done for you; then think and pray about how you can share some of it with one of your mates.

34

Who? An old man who'd lost none of his fire for God
When? At the time Jesus was a baby
Why? Because we need to keep our heads up
Where? Luke 2:22–35

Simeon

Have you ever been driving along a road and said something along the lines of 'I've never noticed that massive tower block before!'... only to discover it's the biggest building in the UK and that it's been there for 20 years?

OK, so I'm exaggerating, but you know what I'm talking about. All too often we miss the profound and the utterly amazing because we are walking around with our heads down.

Perhaps we've done the same with the story of Simeon. This is one of the most amazing brief encounters in the Bible – but most of the time we miss it. When did you ever hear a sermon on Simeon? Enough said. Let's meet him.

Basically Simeon was an old man who knew that his life was incomplete.

These days we strive for early retirement and a life on the golf course, with the odd cruise thrown in for good measure. Or a villa in Spain.

Not Simeon!

A life of leisure was nowhere on his horizon. He was a man in waiting... waiting for peace, waiting for Israel's salvation, waiting to see God's promise to him fulfilled, waiting for the Messiah of the world. The promise God made him personally was simple: he would not die until he saw the Messiah face to face!

This man in waiting was a man of the old school – the school of focused devotion and prayer. We know for a fact that the Holy Spirit was resting powerfully upon him and probably every day was an agenda of more prayer and meditation, until the day came when he would at last clap his eyes on Jesus.

Then one day it happened. Compelled by the Holy Spirit, he went to the temple and found himself there just as Jesus was being brought in by his parents to be circumcised, eight days after his birth. As soon as Simeon saw him he knew this was it. It's described in only one or two verses but the moment is electric.

Have you ever had a moment when you just know that what is happening is going to change everything? Like spotting a job advert and just knowing it's for you? Or seeing a girl across a room and knowing instantly that she's the one?

Well, magnify those moments by a million! Imagine you were Simeon. All those years of waiting, and that day you know the Messiah is going to come into the temple. And then you see him! Gathering Jesus into his arms and probably with his eyes full of tears, Simeon pronounced a startling prophecy over Jesus' life.

It's no soft message. It's not coated in sugar and dressed up in fluff. He predicts that Jesus will be spoken against and that Mary's heart will be pierced by a sword. It's the first clue to Mary that Jesus is going to suffer and die and break her heart.

That's some message to receive when you are holding a baby of only eight days old, and some message to have to deliver to his parents. But Simeon, man of devotion, was chosen for the job. And once that divinely appointed job was done, he knew he could die in peace.

I had a dream once, the night before I was to conduct a funeral. The family had wanted me to give a message about heaven. I admit to feeling more than a little anxious about it.

After a restless few hours, I fell into a deep sleep and had an amazingly vivid dream. In this dream I was a boy again. I know this because I was dressed in the same blue stripy socks, white shorts and top my mum once dressed me in! (Photographic evidence of the offending items safely stashed away.)

As the dream progressed, my life slowly unfolded: my first job, getting married, having children and all the accompanying ups and downs. Then suddenly I was looking right into the eyes of a very old man who was looking tired, frail and near death. It was me, looking into a mirror! I felt shocked at how fast my life had gone past, and now I was facing the ultimate experience of death. Then I woke up.

I was completely disorientated for a few minutes. I knew God was speaking to me and so I asked him what he was showing me. Then I realised.

One day I will draw my last breath and die. And then I will open my eyes again – to find that now I really am alive! I mean **really** alive... **really** living, because I will be with God! And this life, with all its experiences, all its ups and downs, its triumphs and disasters, agonies and ecstasies, will be gone. It will be as if I have woken from a dream.

The point is this. Simeon knew what it was all about and he stayed focused on God. He had his eyes fixed on heaven and on God's purposes. Don't be a man who has your head so far down that you miss the point of what it's all about.

Be a Simeon and discover God's plan for your life. Then go to it with determination and resolve.

QUESTIONS

- Have you asked the Holy Spirit what your life's purposes are?
- Are you man enough for a tough task? Or happy to settle for the quiet life?
- Are you slacking off, waiting quietly for retirement – or living fully with the determination to see God's purposes worked out?

ACTIONS

- Ask God to forgive you if you're walking around with your eyes down or taking your ease when you shouldn't be.
- Determine to fix your eyes on the reality of heaven and work as if you'll be there soon.

35

Who? A desperate man, facing isolation and death
When? In the time Jesus was healing people, around AD 30
Why? We've got so much to learn about being thankful
Where? Luke 17:11–19

The grateful man

A few years after becoming a follower of Jesus, I was just about to start my first full-time job in London. I had finished my studies at uni and had managed to land a sales job for a large bank.

Life was peachy. I had a gorgeous girlfriend – now my significant other half – and a job that paid well. It was a chance to live the London lifestyle, with no kids and no mortgage round my neck. I had a set of wheels with a decent stereo, some good clothes and enough money to scoot away on holiday when I wanted to. Things were looking good!

I was going to a small and fairly old-fashioned church at the time. The congregation were on the whole much older than me and took life far more seriously, but they really kept my feet on the ground.

Let me tell you about Maurice. He was a silver-haired bloke, tall and imposing in a nice Christian kind of way, if you know what I mean. One day at church Maurice came over and congratulated me on landing my new job. I started to unfold in detail just how amazing I had been in the interview process – which, I might add, had involved hundreds of applicants and quite a few interviews for a handful of places. I didn't get too far. Maurice fixed me with a stern glare and said, 'Yes, but don't forget Who you need to thank for getting you the job.' And yes, he really did say 'Who' with a capital 'W'!

Of course, I smiled nicely at Maurice – before walking away feeling really cheesed off.

Of course I knew who to thank!

Me!

I had filled in the forms. I had endured the interviews. I had dazzled them with my unforgettable wisdom and charm! It was all about me! Not God!

I just didn't get it.

Another time I was given a lift in a ropey old car by a church youth worker who told me how grateful he was to God for giving him the car! I reminded him that actually it was because he had a job and saved money that he had a car. I also told him that if God only gave him that old Morris Marina, then God didn't have much taste and I certainly wouldn't be grateful!

Had a lot to learn, didn't I?

Perhaps that's the same attitude we see in the ten leprosy sufferers in Luke 17.

After receiving their healing they all walk away without saying thank you, apart from one man! And that man wasn't even a Jew but an outsider, a Samaritan, someone the Jews would have looked down on.

Remembering God and living a life of thankfulness to him is a profound key to feeling well in your soul! Not only that, it pleases God immensely.

I think we are in real danger of forgetting that it is only because God chooses to sustain us moment by moment that we are even alive. We take the air we breathe for granted, not to mention the food in our cupboards or the clothes on our backs. Frankly, as soon as we start to think it's all about us we are on a slippery slope that ends in a load of godless muck.

I'm not saying we shouldn't ever get a pat on the back. Nor am I saying that a job well done doesn't deserve a reward. What I am saying is that in the final analysis we need to remember that it's God's grace that puts us where we are.

Also, when the chips are down and everything is going pear-shaped we need to keep the same mindset. Don't ever think that because things are bad we have an excuse to blame God. We don't! Stay thankful. There's always something to be grateful for.

Practise life on the positive side of the thankfulness fence and I assure you things will feel a whole lot better. And you will pull out of the down times more quickly.

So next time your boss chews you off for something and it feels bad, thank God for the fact you have a job!

Somehow I have the feeling that the one man who came back to say thanks went on to have a rather fulfilled life.

QUESTIONS

- Do you take the credit for God's blessings in your life?
- Do you thank God in the good times and the bad?

ACTIONS

- If you are reading this and really suffering from illness, thank God for your life, your carers and your destiny! Thank God that Christ is in you with resurrection power. And fight back.
- If you are reading this and you are going through serious family issues, thank God for the good he has done in the past and thank him in advance for what he will do in the future.
- And if everything's hunky-dory and you are doing just great, don't be like most of those men who were healed and forget where your help came from.

36

Who? **A scumbag taxman who followed Jesus**
When? **About AD 30**
Why? **Because no one's beyond redemption**
Where? **Mark 2:13–17**

Matthew

You know when you are onto something good. You feel it in the pit of your stomach. Sometimes your heart rate goes up. It's a gut feeling that's hard to explain or put into words.

I had that feeling when someone took me aside and asked me if I wanted to go to India with him to 'do some ministry'. I leapt at it. As soon as he asked me I just knew I had to get on that plane with him! Yes, OK, so I probably should have prayed and I probably should have chatted it over with a few people... but sometimes you just know, don't you?

When you get that feeling, what you do with it is up to you. You can walk away or you can jump in with two feet.

That's what you get when you look at the encounter of Levi with Jesus.

You probably know Levi better as Matthew, the author of the first Gospel. He was a tax collector. That meant he got rich through other people's misery. He was a corrupt figure of hate.

Jesus had been around in Capernaum for a bit doing stuff and so Levi knew who Jesus was. His reputation had gone before him as a doer of miracles and a teacher well worth listening to – as opposed to some of the raging lunatic gurus of doom that were often marauding around at the time.

So Levi had probably been sussing Jesus out. He had most likely come to the conclusion that he was the real deal after all. Being the man he was, Levi could probably spot a fraud at 30 paces and knew a Walter Mitty when he saw one; after all, he probably was something of one himself!

So now Jesus comes past and doesn't so much ask the million dollar question as put a blunt proposition before him.

'Follow me.'

Put that in context.

'Follow me' means:

- Leave your life of wealth accumulation.
- Leave behind your friends and your family.
- Leave behind everything you know and trust and start your life over again.
- Oh, and by the way… it will cost you everything.

I guess that was a pit of the stomach moment.

Levi went for it.

What about you? You see, I think we all face moments like that. They don't just come when we first decide to follow Jesus. There are times along the way when he calls us to further adventure and to choose whether to lay everything down to follow him.

Levi changed his name to Matthew and started over. He then went on to pour out his heart for the gospel.

Early church tradition has it that he went as far afield as Ethiopia in his quest to spread the news about Jesus and got martyred by being run through by a halberd (a two-pronged spear) in the city of Nadaba in AD 60.

That's a far cry from being a taxman in Capernaum.

I'm fully aware that some of you out there have had that pit of the stomach moment but let it pass you by. Some of you think that you have lost your moment.

Let me tell you something. The God I serve always finishes what he starts. Always! You may have missed that moment in time but if you sincerely tell him that you will follow him when he calls then he will call you again. God loves to use faithful and willing men. So be one!

Or perhaps you don't want to make the commitment to follow Jesus wholeheartedly and do whatever he asks you. That is your privilege and your choice. All I do know is that on the day you meet Jesus in all his risen glory, you may just feel more than a pang of regret!

There's one more thing I need to say about this. In the eyes of the people, Levi was a complete scumbag. He was the lowest of the low, an extortionist, devoid of compassion for people.

And God chose him.

You might feel like you are carrying more baggage than a 747 and have more history than the British Museum. You might feel that you are beyond any usefulness to God. Be assured that those sorts of feelings are enemy lies. Believe none of it. If he can use Levi and turn his life around then don't be so proud as to think he can't do the same for you!

QUESTIONS

- What does it mean for you to respond to Jesus' 'Follow me'?
- What's holding you back from jumping in with both feet to serve Jesus?

ACTIONS

- Do whatever's necessary to de-clutter your spirit so that you're in a state of readiness to go on an adventure with God.

37

Zacchaeus

Who? **A short bloke who had Jesus as a dinner guest**
When? **In the days when Jesus was walking around the earth doing good**
Why? **A must-read story for anyone who needs God's grace!**
Where? **Luke 19:1–10**

I can tell this story in about three lines.

There's this short bloke in Jericho. He's a corrupt taxman out to mess people up for the benefit of his own lifestyle. He climbs a tree to get a glimpse of Jesus. Jesus tells him to get out of the tree. Jesus goes to his house and has a big slap-up meal with him and all his dodgy mates. Wham! Zacchaeus is sorted out for all time. He gives all the stolen money back – and more. The end.

Well… six and a half lines!

There's two things I want us to get hold of from this story:

- Jesus called Zacchaeus by name.
- He went to his home.

There's power in calling someone by his or her name. Where I grew up everyone had the same name: 'Mate'. In fact, the only time someone used your actual name was if you were in trouble! Whenever I heard 'Carl!' being called out, I knew I was in for it!

Not so with Jesus. He calls us by name for an entirely different reason. He calls us by name because he is for us not against us and knows everything about us. In fact, the Bible says that he has been watching over us since before we were born and knows every day planned for us until the day we die (Psalm 139).

That's got to give you some kind of reassurance, hasn't it? You might be reading this on the train as you go to work, or over a mug of tea before walking out of the door. Wherever you are and whoever you are, Jesus is calling you by name and knows all about your day before you even start it! He knows all the good stuff, all the bad stuff and all the stuff you haven't even done yet... and still calls you by name!

I wonder how Zacchaeus felt when he heard his name being called. It was probably a mixture of feeling pretty unnerved and pretty special.

This encounter tells us something very important... and it's a message that still stands today. When Jesus came, he came for everyone, whether you are a thief, a duke, a dentist or a street cleaner. Zacchaeus knew this the moment he heard his name being called... and he got right out of the tree!

Most people thought Zacchaeus was beyond all help, and frankly there wasn't much love for him in Jericho! But no one is past it, in Jesus' view, and no one is unlovable and that's why he called out to Zacchaeus. Pretty amazing, eh? Don't you just love that about Jesus... he's always going for those no one else wants to know about; always sitting down for dinner with the people others want to avoid. Imagine having Jesus come to your house for dinner. Just incredible! The Son of God, who was there at the beginning of time, actually went to Zacchaeus' house for a bite to eat!

This is even more amazing: Jesus wants to come to your house right now. He wants to be involved in every area of your life and help you get things straight. **He wants to help you to be the man you know you ought to be!** For Zacchaeus, the meal ended up with him giving back everything he had stolen and then some!

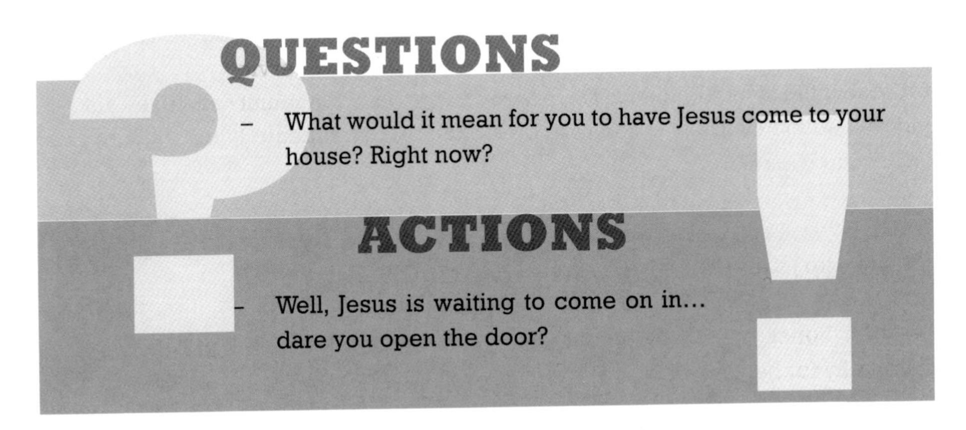

QUESTIONS

- What would it mean for you to have Jesus come to your house? Right now?

ACTIONS

- Well, Jesus is waiting to come on in... dare you open the door?

38

Who? **Leader of the synagogue (the church of those days)**
When? **We're still in the time of Jesus' ministry**
Why? **In the midst of his worst nightmare, he encountered Jesus...**
Where? **Mark 5:21–24,35–43**

Jairus

Jairus' name literally means 'God will enlighten'. Never was a truer name given to a man. When we meet him, Jairus is about to go on a roller coaster ride of emotions, facing every father's worst nightmare and coming through the other side.

The whole encounter is set at the height of Jesus' ministry. There is a profound and divine flow of activity going on. Power is literally pouring out of him. Wherever he goes, stuff happens. Just by being close to Jesus, people are healed. Right in the middle of this particular encounter, a woman merely touches the edge of his cloak and she is healed! Jesus has demonstrated his command over the natural elements and over the demonic – and now he was about to demonstrate his power over death.

So what about Jairus?

We don't know much about the guy. He was a ruler of the synagogue. That means he was a powerful man. He would control the religious services that took place, represent the synagogue to those outside the Jewish community and even act as a judge in disputes. He was a man to be looked up to, respected and honoured. He would have made me nervous. Most serious people do.

Death however respects and honours no man and no man's family and it was just about to rip Jairus' world apart.

Let's be honest, what else can you do in a situation like this but pray and look frantically for help?

JAIRUS

I don't know what Jairus thought about Jesus. We can only guess that the leaders of the synagogue were starting to get a little edgy about him and were probably muttering away in the background. That's what leaders do when a bigger gun arrives on the scene. They get insecure and nervous.

Thing is, when your back's against the wall, all of that rubbish goes out of the window.

Word had got around about Jesus. And Jairus believed. He had nowhere else to go.

That's all it took.

Jesus to Jairus: '**Just believe**.'

He did – and it rocked his world. He got his daughter back and I'm guessing he was never the same again.

In that short space of time he went from the depths of utter despair to the heights of glory.

Jesus to you: '**Just believe**.'

Do you? Or are you too sophisticated?

If there's one thing we learn from Jairus, it's this: It doesn't matter how sophisticated you are; how clever or academic you are; how learned or respected you are. That's what Jairus found out the day he was enlightened.

QUESTIONS

- What worst nightmare have you been in? Did you go to Jesus for help?

ACTIONS

- Next time the chips are down for you, forget all the rubbish about your own abilities or standing. Make Jesus your first port of call. He's always there for you.

39

Who? Astute politician and born survivor
When? Something like AD 33, close to the time of Jesus' death
Why? Because men need backbone
Where? Luke 22:66 – 23:25

Pilate

All too often men try to pass the buck. For a quiet life. Or to protect their corner. For revenge. Or just because…

Have you ever watched one of those reality shows where only the fittest survive, such as *The Apprentice*? Have you noticed how, when people are in a tight corner, everyone tries to ditch the blame? It's startling how people who were patting each other on the back one minute are stabbing each other in the same place less than five minutes later!

Pretty distasteful behaviour. You see it everywhere, from the football pitch to the boardroom. People just looking out for number one.

Let me tell you: **that sort of behaviour is completely incompatible with following Jesus.** When we finally meet the Lord, that kind of track record could be our undoing.

So what about Pilate? You could say that Pilate was in a 'lose/lose' situation. It's one thing to preside over a court of law, but to pass judgement in the kind of situation in which Pilate found himself was something else.

Take a look at the proceedings as described in Luke 23.

First Pilate asks the question: 'Are you the king of the Jews?'

I think at this moment Pilate is just doing his bit and playing to the crowd. So when Jesus says, 'Yes, I am… ' Pilate thinks, 'Well, OK then, that's fine, I asked the question, I got an answer!' All he wants to do is let him go and get out of there. The quiet life beckons!

But once again the people kick off and let it slip that Jesus came from Galilee. Pilate has his way out! If Jesus started his troublemaking in Galilee then it's Herod's problem and not his. Round one to Pilate, who probably retired for a glass of red!

But Herod doesn't get anywhere with Jesus and packs him off back to Pilate, who gets everyone together and tells them there is no charge against Jesus. But, as you can read for yourself, the crowd bays for blood! Even with the promise that Pilate would have Jesus punished (read here: grotesque, incredibly violent beating) the crowd still want Jesus to be nailed to a cross.

And so what does Pilate do? There is no basis for a charge. No basis for the death penalty. Not really even a basis for a beating! Well... Pilate has him killed. Why? Because he wasn't his own man. He was more concerned for his popularity and longevity than for justice.

In John's account (John 19) we get to listen in to a really amazing conversation between Pilate and Jesus. It takes place behind closed doors, just as Pilate is starting to get scared.

- Pilate: 'Where do you come from?'

- Jesus: No answer.

- Pilate: 'Don't you realise that I have the power to have you set free or killed?'

- Jesus (looking Pilate in the eye): 'You would have no power over me if it hadn't been given to you from above!'

That's a killer response from Jesus. What he was saying is this: 'You may think you have the upper hand. You may think you are in control. But the truth is you are part of something much bigger. Bigger than you can ever imagine. In reality, Pilate, I hold all the keys to this situation... '

Scary stuff!

From that moment, Pilate really wanted Jesus set free. In fact, he probably wanted to do a runner! He just had no backbone. In the final analysis, he was not his own man. As soon as the mob shouted, 'You are no friend of Caesar!' Pilate caved in.

Popularity and survival before justice and truth!

I once knew two men who worked in a factory under a real bully. Both were believers. One, the older man, had been a believer for years and never said anything to his boss – preferring to slap him on the back and tell him how great he was.

The younger man had only just become

a Christian. In the past he'd thought that the boss's bullying was a bit amusing – as long as he wasn't on the receiving end! But when he became a believer, he went straight up to his boss and told him what he thought, much to the older believer's shame. In fact, the younger guy just couldn't understand why his colleague had never said anything for all those years. He told him to his face that one of the reasons he had held back from making a decision to follow Jesus was the other guy's conduct towards the boss! How gutting would that feel… to hear that said to you?

As statesman Edmund Burke said, 'All that is necessary for the triumph of evil is that good men do nothing.'

The quiet life comes at what cost?

QUESTIONS

- Before we start to get a bit tough on Pilate, we need to do a frank and honest assessment of our own lives. How many times have we not told the truth because, frankly, it's easier to be the nice guy? Are you your own man, or a crowd follower?
- How many times have we let something wrong continue in the workplace because we don't want a bad work review or face losing our job?

ACTIONS

- Don't be a Pilate! Get stuck in and do your bit.

Who? **A disabled man in Jerusalem for whom Jesus was the only hope**
When? **Again AD 30ish**
Why? **It's good to know no one's a lost cause**
Where? **John 5:1–15**

The disabled man

Life for this guy must have been hell on earth.

If you were crippled, blind, deaf or disabled in any way in the first century, you were stuffed. There is no other way to put it. It was 'game over'.

This disabled man's only hope was the pool at Bethesda, which had legendary healing powers, but even then it was a lost cause because, as you can see from the Bible passage, he couldn't even get to it!

To Jesus it was just a matter of giving the command – and he was instantly healed!

So why did Jesus choose to heal him at this point in time? And what did it feel like for this guy?

Let's ignore the indignation of the religious rulers who got the hump because it happened on the Sabbath! Let's get under the skin of the story.

After this miracle, I believe something happened to this healed guy's inner man as well as the outer because there was no silencing him: he went away telling the Jews that it was Jesus who healed him.

And the healing was undeniable. For 38 years he had been crippled. Maybe for most of that time he had been around the pool. Certainly, he wouldn't have been able to travel far. He would have been well known and seen as a lost cause… or frankly, not any kind of cause!

But Jesus demonstrated that no one was a lost cause.

What does that mean for you?

- Jesus loves you and wants you to be whole.
- Your changed life is a profound witness that Jesus is a miracle worker!
- You are not a lost cause… and no matter what you **feel**, Jesus believes in you.

QUESTIONS

- What does it feel like to know that you are definitely not, no way, a lost cause?
- But check out Jesus' final words of warning to the healed man: 'Stop sinning or something worse may happen to you' (5:14). Is Jesus talking about hell here? Or is he saying that sin led to the condition?

ACTIONS

- We can each come to our own view of that question. The bottom line, as I see it, is that it's best to keep short accounts and lead a repentant, joyful, positive life.

41

Who? Disciple of Jesus
When? Died around AD 65ish
Why? He is a very real encouragement to us all
Where? Lots about him in all four Gospels, plus there are two letters from him in the New Testament

Peter

Peter is famous for three things:

- Messing up.
- Walking on water.
- Being a giant of the early Church.

He is a prime example of what it means thoroughly to mess up and then come really good.

First some facts:

- When you read the Bible, this man is variously called Simon, Simon Peter, Cephas and Peter. Confused?
- Before he started to follow Jesus he was a fisherman.
- He came from a place called Bethsaida (John 1:44).
- His brother was another disciple called Andrew, who had initially followed John the Baptist.
- We know he was married because Jesus healed his mother-in-law! (Matthew 8:14–17).
- He was the only disciple to walk on water like Jesus.
- He denied Jesus three times (John 18).
- Jesus forgave him (John 21:15–19).

PETER

I want us to focus on an area of Peter's life that doesn't get much scrutiny: what might have happened between the cry of the rooster marking Peter's third denial of the arrested Jesus and the moment of his restoration by the resurrected Jesus.

We know that Peter was passionate, aggressive and spontaneous by nature. He was the one who had drawn his sword against Malchus, the high priest's servant (John 18:10) and cut his ear off. He wasn't afraid of confrontation.

He was also the disciple who declared that he was prepared to die for Jesus (John 13:37). He always wanted an answer and wasn't afraid to speak out what everyone else was thinking. His was the name that always appeared first in any list of disciples, highlighting his role as natural leader.

So what happened? How did it all go wrong? Why did he deny his Lord?

When he was in a tight corner, when it really counted, he lost his nerve. Despite all his brashness and confidence, when he was staring at the possibility of execution if identified as one of Jesus' followers, he couldn't tough it out.

How many of us could?

For Peter, it was the beginning of an utter nightmare. He would see Jesus being executed and experience the depths of human despair and grief.

I think in the days between Jesus' crucifixion and Peter's restoration, Peter went through a personal hell.

During that time he confronted more than failure. He faced his lack of moral courage, his lack of integrity, his failure as a man to hold the line. He had to face the fact that fear had got the better of him. And, crucially, he had to face that he had turned his back on the man he considered to be his closest friend, brother, leader and mentor.

That's a lot for a man to have to handle and would drive many of us to the edge of a breakdown, if not all the way into one. Peter was probably feeling shell-shocked and dead inside. All he could do to keep himself going was to try and seek some routine and normality.

So he went fishing.

And so in John 21, in the early hours of the morning, we see Simon Peter out in his boat. All his hopes had been shattered; everything he believed himself to be had been torn to shreds. He was probably struggling in his relationships with the other disciples and just trying to get through each day. Those of us who have been through a very dark time will recognise the feelings.

Then he sees Jesus on the shoreline.

Without hesitation (Peter's famous trait) he jumps in the water and wades to the beach. What follows is an epic conversation with Jesus that has had more diverse opinions expressed about it than 'Who shot JR?'

What's important is this:

- Jesus asks three times if Peter loves him.
- Three times he says he does.
- Three times of saying 'yes' trumps three times of saying 'no'.
- Jesus sees right into Peter's heart.
- Peter is restored.

Now he has confronted the dark centre inside and comes out fighting.

In Acts (the book of exploits of the early believers after the death and resurrection of Jesus), Peter is a different man.

- He preaches a sermon and thousands get saved.
- He walks up to a disabled man and proclaims him healed – and he was, instantly.
- He fronts up to the Sanhedrin (the religious rulers) without fear.

No denying Jesus now!!

Acts 4:13 says it all: 'When they saw the courage of Peter and John and realised they were unschooled, ordinary men, they were astonished and they took note that these men had been with Jesus.' Peter becomes so powerful in God that people even try to throw themselves under his shadow to be healed (Acts 5:15).

This is a very different man.

This was a man who thought he was prepared to die for Jesus but ended up running away from him. Now he was truly prepared to die for him and serve him no matter what.

Jesus said, 'Greater love has no one than this, that one lay down his life for his friends' (John 15:13). Historical sources say that Peter was crucified. They say that he was nailed to a cross upside down.

While Judas got sorry for himself, Peter repented.

If there's one thing to learn from this story it's this: God looks at our potential. He is gracious and forgiving. To those of us who face our failures and weaknesses he grants strength and restoration to be the men we know we ought to be.

QUESTIONS

- Guys, some of us have seized up because we think we have let God down or have denied him in the way we have been living and behaving. Is that your experience? Have you got the courage to face up to your inner darkness and ask God to clean you up?

ACTIONS

- Make today the day you decide really to live for him.
- Make today the day you stop denying him or shying away from who you really are when people ask you.

Who? **Disciple of Jesus who was the team treasurer**
When? **At the time of Jesus**
Why? **We all get tempted to put our own agenda first**
Where? **Luke 22:1–6**

Judas

Lots of people think Judas Iscariot was a fan of direct action, that he was fed up with the Roman occupation and was looking for a punch-up.

Like many at the time, maybe he saw Jesus as a future leader of an armed uprising. During his time with Jesus he was the keeper of the purse, responsible for the disciples' expenses and for giving to the poor. This was an honourable position which indicates to us that he was probably outwardly a trustworthy guy.

But Judas had his own agenda and when he saw it wasn't going to come good, he sold out. For a bag of silver.

He sold out the King of Kings for the amount of money that it took to buy a slave. But as soon as Judas had sold out, he knew he had messed up in a big way! Cut to the heart, he tried to undo the deal (Matthew 27:3–10). Filled with remorse and regret, he tried to return his 30 pieces of silver to the chief priests. He failed in that, so tied a rope around a tree and hanged himself in a field.

As I read it, I see two major lessons. Firstly: Don't pursue your agenda; pursue God's.

We all have ideas about what should happen and how things should be. My advice is to submit those ideas and plans to God. It might be that your ideas are just that – **yours**.

Judas entered into Jesus' service on his own terms and it ruined him. He was probably frustrated and angry. And then he let his heart get corrupted. Then he sold out.

The second lesson I draw from the story of Judas is this: Regret and remorse are wholly different from repentance.

Many times as a pastor I've had people come to me because they have messed up. They wanted to feel better about it and move on. I've realised that not all of these people are repentant; some are remorseful.

There's a big difference.

When you are remorseful, you major on self-pity. It's a 'woe is me' thing. Repentance is something much more positive. Repentance means you want to turn around. It means you know that primarily you have offended God.

That's the difference between a guy like Judas and a man like Peter who you read about on page 112.

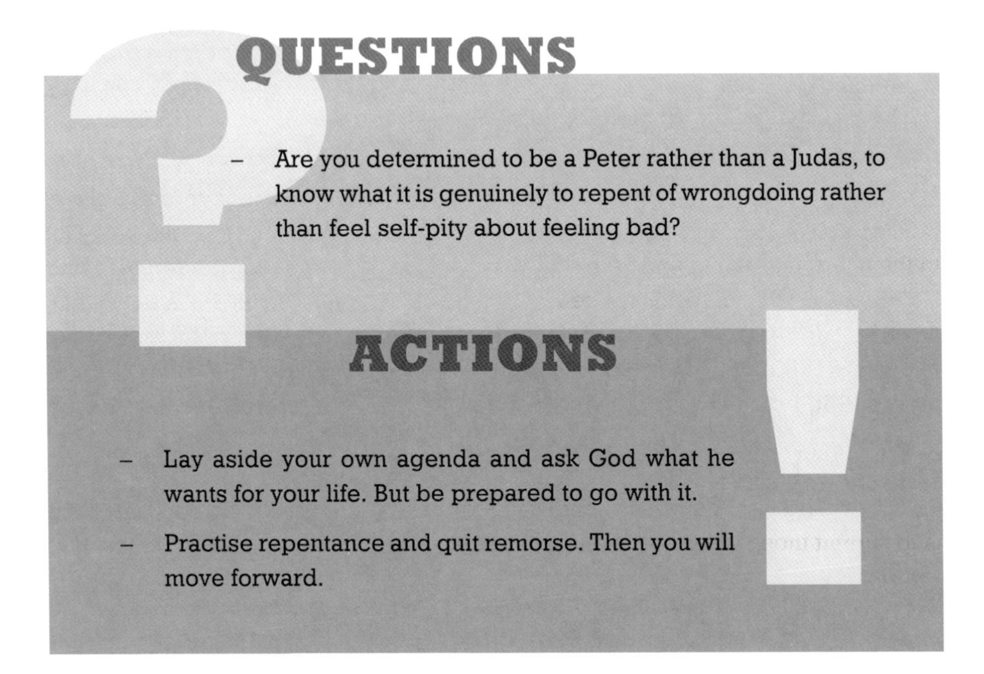

QUESTIONS

- Are you determined to be a Peter rather than a Judas, to know what it is genuinely to repent of wrongdoing rather than feel self-pity about feeling bad?

ACTIONS

- Lay aside your own agenda and ask God what he wants for your life. But be prepared to go with it.
- Practise repentance and quit remorse. Then you will move forward.

43

Who? **A typical bloke**
When? **At the time Jesus was on earth**
Why? **We can identify so much with his cynicism and doubt**
Where? **John 20:24–31**

Thomas

Over the years I have realised that men have two massive enemies when it comes to faith: cynicism and doubt.

When a woman walks into a room of people, she:

a) looks for people to talk to;

b) starts talking;

c) makes a new friend every few minutes;

d) leaves with 15 invites to pamper parties, one to the high street for a latte, and five for dinner 'with your partner'.

Conversely, when a man walks into a room full of people he:

a) plans an escape route and exit strategy;

b) works out his position in the pecking order;

c) pretends to make a new friend but secretly views them with suspicion, doubting everything he's being told;

d) leaves having pretended to make some new mates who he doesn't plan to talk to again ever, until he accidentally bumps into one of them in the High Street 15 years later and kicks off the conversation exactly where they left off.

Doubt and cynicism are great enemies of the faith and men are plagued with them.

Whether it's buying a car, booking a holiday or choosing a builder, men quite often suspect the worst and can't believe what they are told. Sometimes that's a good thing. When it comes to the work of the kingdom, it's a killer. The Bible says, '... without faith it is impossible to please God' (Hebrews 11:6). Not much room there for a life of doubt and unbelief.

Thomas had walked with Jesus. He had seen what Jesus could do. It wasn't as if he was coming to things cold. Far from it. But check out his reaction to having missed out on the stunning sight of the resurrected Christ appearing to the disciples: 'Unless I see... ' Now this is grace and love. Jesus appears later, as if expressly to encourage Thomas to believe.

QUESTIONS

- After the episode of Thomas expressing his doubt, Jesus said, '... blessed are those who have not seen and yet have believed... ' How could you build up muscles of faith? Where in your life can you see an opportunity for that kind of exercise?

ACTIONS

Practise all of the following until they're second nature:

- Give people the benefit of the doubt.
- Choose to be believing not unbelieving.
- Think the best first and not the worst.
- Step out in faith rather than stand back in analytical silence.
- Be a man of the 'why not?' and not the 'what if?'

And live the adventure...

44

Who? **Twelve pretty ordinary guys – at least, to begin with**
When? **AD 30–60ish**
Why? **They rocked the nations**
Where? **The whole book of Acts for starters**

The band of brothers

These guys were amazing. The Bible tells us a fair bit about how they were called to Jesus, what they did as they travelled with him and what they did after he'd been raised from death. Historical documents fill in for us what happened to them later. And it's their ends rather than their beginnings I want us to look at.

ANDREW

A fisherman and brother to Peter. A basic, ordinary kind of guy who was on a search, like so many of us, for fulfilment. He started off following John the Baptist but then met Jesus. He is said to have been crucified on an X-shaped cross because he didn't feel worthy to die the same way as Jesus. Today we know this as the St Andrew's Cross.

BARTHOLOMEW (probably also called NATHANAEL)

Some say this disciple came from a royal background. His family line goes back to King David. Tradition says he preached in Armenia and then on to India where he was put to death by being flayed alive with knives.

JAMES THE ELDER

Another fisherman, and brother to John. His preaching career was cut short around AD 44 when Herod had him put to death 'with the sword' (Acts 12:1,2). He was the first of the twelve to die for his faith.

JAMES THE YOUNGER

James was a fiery, full-on disciple. Tradition says he was crucified in Egypt and his body was sawn into pieces.

THE BAND OF BROTHERS

JOHN

Another fisherman, he was known as the 'beloved disciple'. He was a man of action and huge ambition. Over time he was mellowed by the love of God. Banished to the isle of Patmos, God gave him a vision, from which he wrote Revelation. He was later freed and died a natural death.

JUDAS

Judas Iscariot betrayed Jesus for 30 pieces of silver and afterwards hanged himself. Read about him in more detail on page 116.

JUDE

Jude was a brother of James the Younger. He started off as an angry nationalist. But, consumed with the love of God, he preached his heart out and died a martyr in Persia after being shot with arrows.

MATTHEW

Matthew was a tax collector till Jesus called him. Legend has it that he died a martyr, possibly in Ethiopia.

PETER

Peter was another fisherman. More about him on page 112. He was probably martyred by being crucified upside down.

PHILIP

Philip became a dynamic evangelist and preacher and died a martyr at Hierapolis. Some say he was crucified, others say they hanged him. While he was dying, it's said he asked for his body to be wrapped in papyrus and not linen because he wasn't worthy enough to have his body treated as Jesus' body was.

SIMON

Simon the Zealot was once a nationalist who would have killed for his cause. He was so transformed by Jesus that he ended up giving his life in crucifixion instead.

THOMAS

Thomas, the one-time doubter, is described more on page 118. Some sources say he took the gospel to Persia and India, and was killed by the spears of four soldiers after 20 years of work in India.

So, there you have it. Out of 12 men, 10 died as martyrs, one committed suicide, just one died of natural causes.

After three years of training under Jesus, 11 of them went out into the world with a message that totally changed it. Shaped, moulded and empowered by the Holy Spirit, they rocked the nations.

Something of a challenge, isn't it?

When you next read in a Gospel about these guys getting gathered up by Jesus and following him around, just think about where they ended up. And then think about how Jesus has gathered us up and put us in our places of work, our homes, colleges, towns, cities and villages. There are more of us than there were of them. We are tasked to do even greater things!

Sobering thought.

Better get on with it then, hadn't we?

QUESTIONS

- Do you identify with the personality of any disciple in particular? Or with any of the specific challenges that they faced?

ACTIONS

- What a difference it would make if all across our country believing men stood shoulder to shoulder with each other! How transformational it would be if we became a movement of men who lived for Jesus with every ounce of our strength… choosing to take the hit, and fight in the frontline of the faith battle. For too long we have abdicated our responsibilities and failed to be a band of brothers. For far too long we have let Christian women hold the line in prayer and mission. Time to get going…

45

Who? Young man with the world at his feet
When? AD 30s
Why? His dialogue with Jesus cuts to our hearts today
Where? Mark 10:17–22

The rich yuppie

It's so easy to look at the Bible and count yourself out of the equation while sitting in smug judgement!

This is one of those stories we love to put a spin on so that it doesn't push us too far.

In brief:

Man walks up to Jesus; tells Jesus he is cutting the mustard on every level. As for him, he lives the Ten Commandments, follows the Law, does all the right stuff.

So Jesus does his normal thing. Cuts to the heart of the matter.

'OK, that's great! Really well done! Now go and give all your possessions to the poor and follow me.'

Ouch!

Just when you thought it was safe to be a disciple of Jesus, you get hit by yet another curved ball.

When I first became a follower of the way of Jesus, I took the Bible at face value. Then, after a short period of blissful naivety, the church started to teach me what Jesus really meant when he said these radical things.

- It's all about your heart, Carl...
- As long as you are **prepared** to give it all up, that's the main thing...
- What Jesus **really** meant was that you should have your eyes fixed on him and not the latest stuff... although he won't be that upset if you buy that new Bang & Olufsen plasma...

What a load of rubbish! Jesus knew what he meant.

And he's been making people feel uncomfortable ever since.

I've been trying my best to take God at his word. It's been an adventure… and I'm still learning. I'm doing my best to hold everything lightly… in the certain knowledge that everything we have belongs to God anyway – not just the classic ten per cent.

One day I met a couple who had a very talented daughter and were short of money to be able to put her through college. As I left the house, the Lord said to me, 'You have £1000 in your account, son.'

'Yes, Lord… but if I give them the money, I won't have any!'

'Just give it, son… '

So I thought I would check it out with the wife!

'Karen, there's this family… '

'Just give them the money… '

'But if I give them the money, we won't have any… '

'Just give it!'

Who am I to disobey both the Lord and my wife!

So, anonymously, I put £1000 through the door.

Our account was empty and we were on a very low income. Scary…

Within four months, in various ways, £3000 had come through our door, keeping us afloat as we planted a congregation. God is amazing!

In my first year of ministry we were only on about £3500 a year. One day we only had £5 in the account and empty cupboards. Karen was more than upset and concerned as we drove home. When we got home there was over £100-worth of groceries on the driveway. We had told no one about our situation. Baked beans had never tasted so good. God is incredible!

On another occasion I gave my coat to a down-and-out who turned up at the church. That makes me sound heroic, but he dropped about ten hints about how nice my jacket looked before I cottoned on! It left me with no coat on a rainy day. That evening I was watching the telly with Karen when she pointed out a man wearing an expensive-looking three-quarter length black suede jacket that she said would look good on me.

The doorbell went.

Standing there was a new believer from the church holding a bag. 'This is for you,' she said. 'It doesn't fit my boyfriend but I thought it might fit you… '

You guessed it…

Karen nearly passed out when I walked in the lounge like the Fonz…

'Hey… check it out!'

God is all-sufficient. Or, in the words of Jesus, '… do not worry about … what you will eat or drink … seek first his kingdom and his righteousness, and all these things will be given to you as well' (Matthew 6:25–33).

Seek first the kingdom!

When you do… it's dynamite!

OK, so you tell me we can't all make ourselves homeless and give all our clothes away. I hear you. Yes, the stuff/possessions in themselves are not the issue. It's what we're seeking after that counts. But the fact is, we could go way further than we do. That large bank balance sitting there doing nothing may one day seem quite horrific when we face Jesus.

When Alexander the Great died, he asked to be put in an open coffin with his palms open to show that while he had conquered the known world he left it with nothing. Wise man.

QUESTIONS

- The rich young ruler may have come good… we just don't know. But how do you think you would react in his shoes to Jesus' challenge?
- Are you fixing your eyes on what's to come? Or on what's in Curry's catalogue?

ACTIONS

- Live dangerously! Embrace the adventure of open-handed, generous faith.
- Be a true servant of the living God.

46

Who? **A new believer in the early Church**
When? **AD 35ish**
Why? **It's a very sobering lesson**
Where? **Acts 5:1–11**

Ananias

The story of Ananias unnerves me. It's not pleasant. But we ignore it at our peril.

This is a story for those people who say that since the death and resurrection of Jesus, God doesn't deal with sin in the same way as he once did. It's a story for those who are keen on preaching a message of grace and love – missing out the bit about judgement.

This happened in a period of the early Church when everyone was sharing their possessions and no one was without food. People were open-handed with what God had given them. We talk about tithing – but they were into sharing in a big way, with everything held 'in common'. No, really! I'm talking about being completely open with possessions so that no one went without. If there was a need, you just gave stuff away! I like that. There's no reason for followers of Jesus to behave any other way.

It was becoming a widespread practice among the believers to sell stuff and lay the proceeds at the feet of the church leaders.

That's what Ananias did… sort of.

The problem wasn't that he held something back.

But that he pretended that he was giving everything.

The massive problem was that his pastor was Simon Peter who at the time was moving under a powerful anointing from God. When the Lord exposed the lie, Ananias just dropped down dead. We don't know if it was fear that caused him to die or whether it was sovereign judgement.

This wasn't the first time the Bible records that kind of thing happening. There was, for example, a man called Uzzah who died for putting his hand on the Ark of the Covenant (see 2 Samuel 6). And in Leviticus 10 we read of two brothers, Nadab and Abihu, who made an inappropriate offering and got burned up by fire.

What does this tell us?

It tells us that God is not to be mocked.

He hates deceit. He likes our 'yes' to be 'yes' and our 'no' to really mean 'no'. He likes us to be upfront and honest. He likes us to be honourable and noble.

When we are less than that, there can be consequences.

If Ananias had been straight with Peter, he would have lived. Ironically, his name means, 'God has dealt graciously'.

QUESTIONS

- Are you missing out on God's best because of dishonesty? I won't push it too far, but I'm convinced that many of us miss out on the blessing God has for us because we aren't straight and honest. Integrity is everything. Smith Wigglesworth, a preacher and great performer of signs and wonders in the early twentieth century, reckoned that personal integrity was one of the keys to seeing the power of God.

ACTIONS

- Keep straight accounts with God and I can guarantee that your life will come under the blessing of God. More than that, it's great to wake up every morning with a completely clean conscience.

Who? Forgotten hero of the early Church
When? We're still around AD 35 or 40
Why? He stood up for what he believed – and paid the ultimate price
Where? Acts 6 and 7

Stephen

Stephen had it all:

- He was full of the Holy Spirit.
- He performed miracles.
- He was a brilliant communicator.
- He didn't back down.
- He fronted out an angry mob.
- He died speaking out for what he believed.
- He was, at heart, a servant.

He's something of a hero for me. He has all the qualities I aspire to and yet so dismally fail to live up to.

Until the point of his confrontational sermon, when he stands up against the religious authorities, he's a bit in the shadows.

His job was to ensure the correct distribution of food to the poor. It wasn't high status and it probably meant dealing with all kinds of moaning and complaining. He wasn't upfront, but more of a backroom boy; more concerned with others than himself.

OK, so he performed miracles... but somehow you get the feeling that he wasn't a showman in a big white suit. He just quietly got on with serving the poor and praying for the sick and because of his humble heart and faith-filled prayers, God used him as a conduit to do some amazing stuff.

I'm always wary of people who push themselves forward. Maybe they do so out of insecurity, maybe its uncrucified ambition. Much better to wait until God shines his light on you.

'He is genuinely great who considers himself small and cares nothing about high honours... ' (Thomas à Kempis).

I wonder at which point Stephen realised that his life was in danger.

Whatever, we don't see any hesitation or backing down. Whether he lived or died was secondary. Jesus was everything.

The reality of God's love may seem incompatible with suffering and martyrdom. But what's clear to me in this account is that, just before Stephen's murder, God cocooned him in his presence. I find the account of his death among the most moving passages in the whole of Scripture.

Let's not coat this in fluff. To be stoned must be a horrific death: broken bones, lacerated skin, torn flesh and heavy blood loss is the order of the day. But during the whole time the crowd went to work on him, Stephen was praying – probably infuriating and inflaming them even more.

Incredibly, he even prayed that his murderers would be forgiven!

Think about that next time someone carves you up on the M6 or tries to derail your career.

Stephen 'fell asleep,' says the Bible. God took him to be with him.

The words of Jesus as he was dying are in my mind. To the thief on an adjoining cross he said, '...today you will be with me in paradise' (Luke 23:43).

QUESTIONS

- Why is it we find it hard to read our Bible on the train? Or offer to pray with a colleague? Or speak up when someone is giving Jesus a verbal going-over?
- Why are we so weak and frankly pathetic when it comes to sharing our faith and standing up for what we believe?
- Stephen didn't consider this life a priority. Nor do I think status, possessions, promotion and accumulating savings were priorities to him.

ACTIONS

- Think about Stephen the next time you clam up when someone asks what you were doing at the weekend.
- Take a long hard look at your priorities and how they might need a bit of attention.

Who? **A man who lived up to his name**
When? **The period of Acts**
Why? **We need to learn about the sheer power of encouragement to bring positive change**
Where? **Lots of mentions throughout Acts, from chapter 4 onwards**

Barnabas

Bear with me for a bit of history; it's relevant, I promise!

In June 1940, Britain was at war with Nazi Germany. It was a bleak time. The allies had suffered a very serious setback. The British Expeditionary Force in France had been routed and lost its equipment. The French divisions had been hammered badly. It seemed that all was lost. Prime Minister Winston Churchill addressed Parliament – a masterclass in how to motivate and encourage a nation.

His speech began: 'I spoke the other day of the colossal military disaster which occurred when the French High Command failed to withdraw the northern armies from Belgium at the moment when they knew that the French front was decisively broken at Sedan and on the Meuse. This delay entailed the loss of 15 or 16 French divisions and threw out of action for the critical period the whole of the British Expeditionary Force… the battle in France has been lost … They (the soldiers) have suffered severely… '

Where do you go from there?

The British army was shattered, demotivated and exhausted. Veterans of the Dunkirk rescue rarely speak about their experiences, such was the horror.

Within minutes Churchill had finished his speech, concluding with these words: 'What General Weygand called the Battle of France is over. I expect that the Battle of Britain is about to begin. Upon this battle depends the survival of Christian civilisation. Upon it depends our own British life, and the long continuity of our institutions and our Empire. The whole fury and might of the enemy must very soon be turned on us.

'Hitler knows that he will have to break us in this Island or lose the war. If we can stand up to him, all Europe may be free and the life of the world may move forward into broad, sunlit uplands. But if we fail, then the whole world, including the United States, including all that we have known and cared for, will sink into the abyss of a new Dark Age made more sinister, and perhaps more protracted, by the lights of perverted science.

'Let us therefore brace ourselves to our duties, and so bear ourselves that if the British Empire and its Commonwealth last for a thousand years, men will still say, "This was their finest hour".'

Subsequently, the allies stood their ground, re-equipped, and slogged on for the next five years until the Nazi regime was taken down.

There are many reasons why the Allies fought through to victory, and here isn't the place to go into them. What I know, however, is that when I read the whole Churchill speech it lifts me and makes me straighten my back. I can imagine sitting at home at the time of the broadcast, listening to the words from the radio and feeling proud to be British and capable of coming back from disaster. I expect the whole nation felt encouraged to plough on – no matter what. And that's what they did… through the 50,000 civilian deaths during the Blitz, rationing, fear and the loss of loved ones.

Do not underestimate the power of positive words and encouragement.

So to Barnabas. His real name was Joseph, but it was changed to Barnabas, meaning 'son of encouragement'.

Barnabas lived and ministered in tough times as well. It wasn't all rosy in the early years of the Church. Extreme intimidation and martyrdom were ever present as the Church sought to push outwards and spread the message. Tasked with being a missionary, Barnabas would head off into the unknown, with nothing but his faith and his wits to keep him safe.

The thing is, Barnabas was no superstar performer who wrote books that got into the Bible or gave knockout sermons.

But Barnabas believed in encouraging people and wasn't precious about position.

Barnabas brought Paul into the fold and was happy to stand aside to let him take the lead when the time was right. For him, the priority was the kingdom and seeing others encouraged and built up – including Paul! When Paul (known then as Saul) first appeared on the scene, no one wanted to deal with him. He was a slaughterer of believers and viewed with massive suspicion. Barnabas saw beyond the man's past. The rest is history.

He was consistent. Later, he stood up for John Mark when Paul couldn't be bothered with him because he (John Mark) had previously done a runner. Again, choosing to believe in the guy rather than dwell on the past, Barnabas chose to go with John Mark. For the record, Paul came round in the end (2 Timothy 4:11).

Barnabas also encouraged by giving. He sold a piece of property and, without hesitation, gave the money to the disciples (Acts 4:36,37).

And Barnabas encouraged churches. In Acts 11 he goes to Antioch, stirs up the believers, leads loads of people to God and stays there for a year together with Paul – encouraging, teaching and motivating. Barnabas, it says in Acts 11:23, 'encouraged them all to remain true to the Lord with all their hearts'.

When you stay with a group of people for that long, you are telling them that you believe in them. He didn't just say stuff to make people happy. He really lived it.

Here's the key. Barnabas consistently believed the best of people. Just as Churchill really believed the nation could pull through to victory, so Barnabas could look past previous failures and disasters (even murders in Paul's case) and see the potential in people and situations. As we've seen, he put his money where his mouth was.

If we followed Barnabas' example, I think our places of work, our homes and our churches would be different places. If we:

- chose to see the best and not the worst…
- trained ourselves to have a positive first response and not a negative one…
- made a decision to believe the best in every situation and want the best for every person we met…

- died to cynicism, the enemy of encouragement, and embraced a positive mindset…

…then the possibilities for good are endless.

Remember, our words can bring life or destroy. That doesn't mean we always have to agree with everyone. It means we should aim to leave people feeling more positive than they were before we started talking.

QUESTIONS

- Have you had your life impacted by encouragement?
- How encouraging are you to others?

ACTIONS

- As it says in 1 Thessalonians 5:11 – ' ... encourage one another and build each other up.' Make sure that the words coming out of your mouth are positive and build people up.
- Take a look at the Barnabas activities listed above and see how many you can adopt into your lifestyle.

Who? Magician and conjuror
When? Early Church period
Why? Made such a mess of things he got a sin named after him (simony)
Where? Acts 8:9–25

Simon the Sorcerer

It's not every day that you do something so out of order that you get a sin named after you! That's what this guy did.

Though it's hardly a word used much in everyday conversation, the word 'simony' has been derived from his story. The dictionary describes it as 'the buying or selling of pardons, benefits and other ecclesiastical privileges'.

Simon the Sorcerer was much more than a wandering David Copperfield who did a few tricks to wow the crowd. Later he became a hero for a movement known as Gnosticism. Gnostics were people who thought that they had the inside track on the deepest secrets. They thought Simon had great power from God because of his magic tricks. More than that, Acts 8:10 seems to indicate that he was either claiming to be God or God's main representative.

Then he met the apostle Philip and the town of Samaria wasn't big enough for both of 'em.

Philip had come to Samaria to tell people about Jesus. He just wanted people to know the truth.

Simon wanted position and power.

Spiritually that's about as far apart as two people can get.

Sadly, there are many people out there today who want dramatic results to their prayers mainly so that they look holy and spiritual and so that others look up to them.

That's what led to the sin of simony. Simon offered to pay Peter and John to get spiritual power and position. Philip struck the fear of the living God into Simon the Sorcerer. The Bible doesn't tell us what happened to him but other books that never made it into the Bible describe him meeting a nasty end when he tried to outgun Peter.

This is a heart issue. Simon would have done anything to get his hands on the kind of power that Philip was demonstrating. There's no room in the kingdom for that kind of attitude. Everything we do should be for the glory of Jesus, not for us.

As soon as you start wanting to use God for your own gain, you are going to crash and burn in a big way. And yet, still they come from all over the world: preachers and evangelists and doers of miracles looking for fame and fortune – usually in expensive suits that cost more than the people they are preaching to earn in a year. And at the centre of everything they do is them – not Jesus.

And it's not just the big guns either. You see it in local churches and in workplaces… people vying for position, lobbying for power. It's an ugly thing. Have nothing to do with it. Keep yourself humble before God and be content with the life he has given you. If he wants to shine his light on you, well, that's his business… and if he does – stay humble!

QUESTIONS

- Is your life one of substance? Or smoke and mirrors?
- How important is power to you?

ACTIONS

- Examine your heart and your motives before God.
- Take an inventory of your achievements. Weigh them up. Are they for your glory or his?

50

Who? Super-apostle and church planter extraordinaire
When? Died around AD 65
Why? The murderous persecutor of Christians turned evangelist who stormed the ancient world with the gospel
Where? He actually wrote huge chunks of the New Testament so his fingerprints are all over it

Paul

One ancient writer describes Paul as a short, bald, bow-legged and hook-nosed man with eyebrows that met in the middle.

However, as descriptions of people are subjective and as the book this comes from is what we call 'apocryphal', you can't go with that one hundred per cent. Whatever his appearance, he was an incredibly powerful character. The Bible totally bears that out.

In his early life, Paul (otherwise known as Saul) was a scholar. He was born in the Roman city of Tarsus and was a devout Jew. From childhood he was taught the Jewish Scriptures in the synagogue as well as the traditions of his faith. Later, probably as a teenager, he went on to study under a famous rabbi called Gamaliel and it was during this time that Paul became more than 'full on'.

In fact, 'full on' is an understatement. The Bible first mentions Paul when Stephen is getting stoned. Paul is in the background holding the cloaks of the killers. His role was to hunt down Jews who had converted to Jesus and deal with them decisively. So effective was Paul that he was known throughout the emerging Church as a chief persecutor and a man to fear.

Then he met Jesus on the road to Damascus.

And everything changed.

PAUL

From killer of Christians to missionary for Christ, all of Paul's energy and drive then went into love for people and a passion for the gospel. Over the years he covered probably in excess of 13,000 miles in his quest to spread God's Word. He faced imprisonment, beatings, death threats, shipwrecks, floggings, financial hardship and isolation.

Never did he let up and never did he quit.

He undertook five missionary trips over approximately a 35-year span. He stayed for long periods with different people to make sure that the Word of God went deep. During his two years in Ephesus, people got healed just by touching a handkerchief he had touched. In Rome he was finally placed under arrest and martyred.

You can read accounts of his journeys all over the place, and not just in the Bible, but I want to focus on his character.

I think a key to his character is in Colossians 1:29 where he says something astonishing. He's talking about sharing Christ with as many people as possible, and helping them grow as disciples. And he says, 'To this end I labour, struggling with all his energy, which so powerfully works in me.'

I mean, what on earth is going on here?

Here we have a guy who seems to be so overwhelmed with the presence of Jesus that it's almost flooring him. I think it goes a long way to explaining what's happening when people used to touch his apron or handkerchief and get healed.

He simply **overflowed** with the presence of Jesus.

Now here's the thing. I believe that this sort of 'overflow' is within the reach of every one of us.

But it takes sacrifice and single-minded devotion.

We know Paul was an intense kind of guy from the outset. Rigorous and zealous, he was one of life's obsessive characters. And that's not a criticism. God uses obsessive people to break new ground and do extraordinary things. The great adventurer Columbus who discovered America was an obsessive. So is modern-day adventurer Steve Fossett who has broken over 100 world records. He once flew round the world non-stop in a hot air balloon in 67 hours and one minute. These are the sort of men who don't quit. They spit out the grit, dig deep and persist to the bitter end.

Paul's obsessive personality got gripped by Jesus and that upped the ante significantly. Now he was driven by heavenly power. He pursued the glory of God and poured out his life for the gospel. Shunning status, safety and security he funded his way (by making tents) across half the world for the sake of the kingdom. In return, God filled him to overflowing with his power. So much so, that Paul struggled to contain it. I can just see him pacing up and down in his cell or in his quarters, dictating thought and idea after thought and idea as they poured from his heart. Restless, frustrated and passionate… he was one of the great adventurers of his time and, as a result, the gospel spread like wildfire.

Whether it was debating with philosophers in Athens, rulers in Rome or low ranking prison guards in Philippi, Paul was ready to share Jesus. He could speak to anyone, adapting his style to whoever he was speaking to. When he saw a demon he took it on; where he saw sickness he commanded healing; when he was in danger of death he looked to God. He had been given a glimpse of something beyond this life and it changed him forever.

His life inspires me to shake out of my lukewarm apathy.

Bring it on!

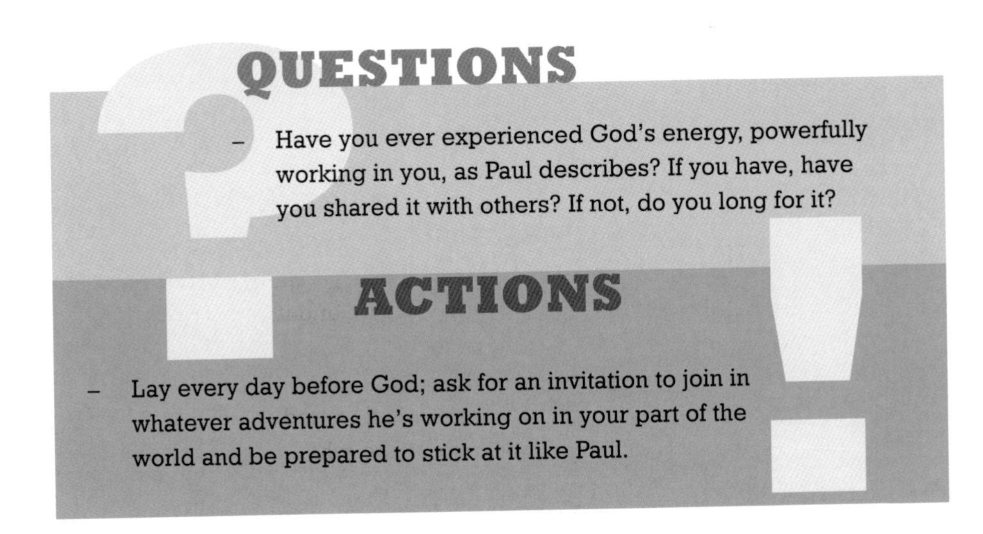

QUESTIONS

- Have you ever experienced God's energy, powerfully working in you, as Paul describes? If you have, have you shared it with others? If not, do you long for it?

ACTIONS

- Lay every day before God; ask for an invitation to join in whatever adventures he's working on in your part of the world and be prepared to stick at it like Paul.

51

Who? A man with a teachable heart
When? AD 60s
Why? For lessons in submission and godliness
Where? Paul wrote two New Testament letters to him

Timothy

As a child, Timothy was taught the Scriptures and the ways of God by his mother and grandmother. Later, Paul played a key part in his conversion to the way of Jesus. That's why Paul refers to him as his son or child in the faith. Paul took his mentoring seriously, inviting Timothy to go with him on his second major mission. I like that – an older guy taking a younger man with him, teaching him stuff on the hoof. We need to see more of that in the churches.

It's here that we first see Timothy's outstanding character and honourable heart. Because his dad was Greek and his mother Jewish, Timothy hadn't been circumcised. Paul knew that it could close doors to the Jewish community if Timothy wasn't circumcised and so – you guessed it – Paul asked Timothy to undergo the procedure (Acts 16:3).

Now think about it… this is a grown man we are talking about! These days we baulk at going on a mission trip if we have to raise a lot of money or have to sleep in places less comfortable than we are used to, or go without TV! Try circumcision as an adult, with no anaesthetic. I'm not trying to be crude or sensationalist. I'm making a point. Timothy had a heart of obedience to Paul and wanted to learn. He was passionate about getting the gospel out there and if there was a potential barrier, he had the heart and will to remove it.

As Timothy grew in God and in spiritual stature, Paul started sending him on some serious trips as his mouthpiece. It got to the stage where Paul trusted Timothy above all others and, as with all good mentoring relationships, Timothy moved from being a child in the faith to a brother. When Paul was up against it and facing death, it was Timothy he asked for, no one else (2 Timothy 4:9). This speaks of a close bond between these two great men of God: one who had been through the fire and the test of time, and one who was raised up to continue the work.

QUESTIONS

- Have you a close mentoring or mentored bond with other men? If you have, do you thank God for those relationships and really value them? If not, what benefits might it give you and others to grow those kinds of relationships?

ACTIONS

There are two areas of action I want to drive home:

- If you are an older man in the faith and have walked with God for a time, then look for younger men you can raise up. It's your duty and responsibility. Help move younger men who are hungry for God into leadership. Take a chance; give them a head of steam; communicate that you believe in them; then stand back and watch what they can do. You might well be surprised. When I was 23, a wise man and father in the faith called Bob Allen took me under his wing. Seven years later I was senior pastor of the church. He believed in me and taught me. It made all the difference.
- If you are a younger man, you would do well to submit intelligently to those who have gone before you. You will grow faster that way and draw closer to God. Listen to what they say, take note of their wisdom and respect their opinions. And when they ask you to do something you find a bit tricky… as long as it is godly and right, just get on with it. Take note of 1 Timothy 4:12: 'Don't let anyone look down on you because you are young, but set an example for the believers in speech, in life, in love, in faith and in purity.' I learned to surround myself with older, wiser men and I still do so to this day. One day, you will be one of the older guys. Then, just remember the slack you were given and the humility with which men dealt with you!

52

Who? King of Kings, our master and commander, our captain
When? He existed before creation and lives eternally
Why? He's the source of all love, all goodness, all life
Where? The whole Bible is his story, from Genesis to Revelation

As King of Kings, he is mighty and powerful and will one day judge the nations.

Yet he is all-forgiving and all-gracious.

He burns with holiness – yet is filled with compassion.

He is the source of all our understanding of the qualities of nobility, heroism, sacrifice, honour, majesty, strength, integrity, mercy, authority, justice, righteousness and morality… and much more.

He is the source of life; Alpha and Omega, beginning and end.

He takes people's lives and turns them around.

He takes the sick and he heals them.

He takes the broken and he makes them whole.

He takes the self-sufficient and shows them their dependence on him.

He humbles the proud and shows mercy to the weak.

He uplifts the poor and challenges the rich.

He touches the untouchable and loves the unlovable.

He always had time for people: the outcast… the prostitute… the small child… the lonely… the sick…

He was there at the beginning and he will be there at the end of time as we know it.

He will throw Satan and his demons into the lake of fire.

And all of us will one day kneel before him.

He laid down his life for you. Taking the pain and the humiliation, he had you in his mind as he died. Yes, you!

He took the hit for all the stuff you have done that is an offence to the God of the universe and he took the hit for all the stuff that you are going to go on to do.

QUESTIONS

- Is that the King you follow?
- Is that the Jesus you serve?
- Are you ready to go where he tells you to go and do what he asks you to do?
- Do you live for him? And I mean, really live for him?

ACTIONS

- Stop being lukewarm.
- Stop making excuses for half-hearted discipleship.
- Shake off your apathy.
- Let go of your pride.
- Yield everything to him: your wallet, your pride, your time, your future, your career, your ego.
- Serve him, honour him and live your life to the full.

As believing men, we are a band of brothers. Let's be iron sharpening iron! Let's pursue the kingdom together!

SPADEWORK

LAYING FOUNDATIONS WITH 52 MEN FROM THE BIBLE

		page
3	Abraham	14
11	Achan	36
1	Adam	7
17	Amalekite soldier	51
46	Ananias	126
44	Band of brothers	120
48	Barnabas	130
7	Bezalel	26
9	Caleb	31
32	Centurion	90
25	Daniel	72
18	David	54
40	Disabled man	110
12	Ehud	38
22	Elisha	64
13	Gideon	40
35	Grateful man	97
30	Habakkuk	86
23	Hezekiah	66
27	Hosea	77
29	Isaiah	83
4	Jacob	17
38	Jairus	105
52	Jesus	141
31	John the Baptist	88
5	Joseph	19

		page
10	Joshua	33
28	Job	79
42	Judas	116
33	Legion	92
36	Matthew	100
19	Mephibosheth	57
6	Moses	23
20	Nathan	59
26	Nebuchadnezzar	75
24	Nehemiah	69
2	Noah	11
50	Paul	136
41	Peter	112
8	Pharaoh	29
39	Pilate	107
45	Rich yuppie	123
14	Samson	43
15	Samuel	46
16	Saul	48
34	Simeon	94
49	Simon the Sorcerer	134
21	Solomon	62
47	Stephen	128
43	Thomas	118
51	Timothy	139
37	Zacchaeus	103

GROUNDBREAKER

Some of the Bible stories from SPADEWORK can be found in a 32-page colour magazine called GROUNDBREAKER, together with three fantastic true stories of men today:

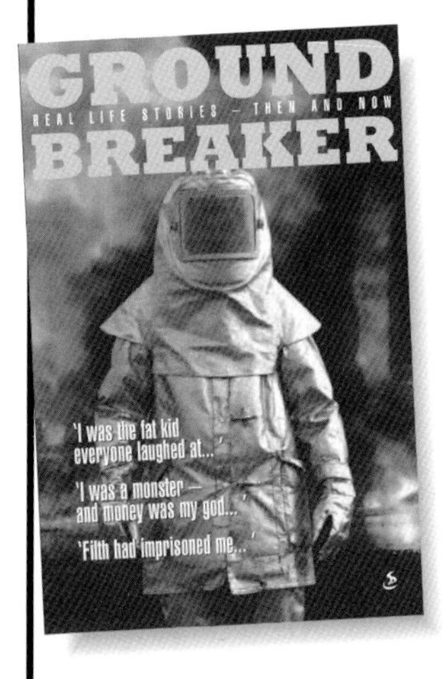

CLIVE was the classic fat kid who was bullied at school. He transformed himself into a martial arts champion with a TV career – but still his life fell apart big time.

JON believed he was invincible. His lifestyle centred on binge drinking, affairs and dodgy business deals. Even a 90 mph car crash that should have wiped him off the planet didn't stop him.

LANCE grew up on a diet of glossy girlie magazines – and porn became a serious addiction that dominated his adolescence, threatened his marriage, and led to years of counselling.

GROUNDBREAKER – not only an ideal 'taster' for SPADEWORK but great to give away to men contacts.

Want to know more?

www.rejesus.co.uk is a great website to explore.

And the guys at the Christian Enquiry Agency (www.christianity.org.uk) can also send you stuff in the post or – if you want – link you up with a local church. Or if you don't fancy church you can be put in touch with a Christian in your area to meet up with for a chat.

THE CHRISTIAN ENQUIRY AGENCY
FREEPOST WC2947
SOUTH CROYDON
CR2 8UZ

Email: enquiry@christianity.org.uk